Invisible Generations

01 02 03 04 05 23 22 21 20 19

Caitlin Press Inc.
8100 Alderwood Road,
Halfmoon Bay, BC V0N 1Y1
www.caitlin-press.com

Text and cover design by Vici Johnstone
Cover image courtesy The Reach, Abbotsford, P20534
Printed in Canada

Caitlin Press Inc. acknowledges financial support from the Government of Canada and the Canada Council for the Arts, and the Province of British Columbia through the British Columbia Arts Council and the Book Publisher's Tax Credit.

Library and Archives Canada Cataloguing in Publication

Invisible generations : living between Indigenous and white in the Fraser Valley / Jean Barman.

Barman, Jean, 1939- author.

Includes bibliographical references and index.

Canadiana (print) 20190131039 | Canadiana (ebook) 20190131055 | ISBN 9781773860053 (softcover) | ISBN 9781773860107 (HTML)

Subjects: LCSH: Kelleher, Irene, 1901-2004. | LCSH: Kelleher, Irene, 1901-2004—Family. | LCSH:

   British Columbia—Ethnic relations. | LCSH: British Columbia—Race relations. | CSH: Native peoples—British Columbia—Social conditions. | CSH: Native peoples—British Columbia—Residential schools—History. | CSH: Native peoples—British Columbia—Ethnic identity. | CSH: Native peoples—British Columbia—Race identity.

LCC E98.E85 B37 2019 | DDC 305.8970711—dc23

INVISIBLE GENERATIONS

Living between Indigenous and White in the Fraser Valley

JEAN BARMAN

CAITLIN PRESS

CONTENTS

"There's nobody to write about us; it will be the first time to tell the story."
—Irene Kelleher

PREFACE

Irene Kelleher wanted her story told, and the time is now. The first drafts were written during the 1990s at the behest of and in collaboration with Irene, who initiated, commented on, and approved the various iterations. Returning to the text after Irene's death and again recently, I fleshed out some of the situations, places, and persons in ways I think Irene would have wanted in order to make her story accessible and explicable to today's readers.

The rightness of the time for publication is prompted by a greater openness in British Columbia and across Canada towards persons of mixed Indigenous and white descent, as Irene was, and by new publications opening up broader perspectives on the history of British Columbia's Fraser Valley, where Irene lived. Chad Reimer's wonderful *Before We Lost the Lake* turned my attention to Caitlin Press, and I thank Vici Johnstone and Holly Vestad for responding positively to my overture. Val Billesberger of the Mission Community Archives kindly tracked down images that bring Irene's story to life.

Invisible Generations is about one woman, her parents and grandparents, and their families and friends who lived in the Fraser Valley in southwestern British Columbia, and it is also about all of us. Irene's story is about real people leading real lives in times past, just as we each do in the present day.

Irene was burdened by history. She lived all her life in the shadow of a past she bore in her physical features, so she considered, and in her every action. It was a past in which she took great pride, especially with respect to her parents' and grandparents' lives, but it was also a past that she felt set her apart from those around her—both in everyday life and in her career as a schoolteacher.

Wherever we live, *Invisible Generations* is an object lesson as to how we should, and should not, behave towards each other. During most of Irene's long life, 1901–2004, and during the lives of her parents and grandparents, racial origins were all too often given priority as markers of acceptance, or not, by others. To live well between Indigenous and white, as these three generations of a Fraser Valley family and their closest friends did, was not easy. The first generation resembled many of the families around them, originating with a white man and an Indigenous woman. There were fewer such families in the second and third generations, with the arrival of growing numbers of white women to partner with white men. The lives of these three generations, and of their friends and neighbours, embodies a message for all of us that, while we cannot undo the past, we can learn from it and behave as best we can towards each other.

Along with Irene, my understanding of early Fraser Valley families has been enriched by conversations over the years with Lenora Battel, Donna Beaumont, Anita Bonson, Fred Brachus, Laura Buker, Pat Campo, Heather Commodore, Jane Cromarty, Denise Douglas, Rosemarie George, Jacqueline Gresko, Pauline Harris, Ronald and Jean Foote Humphreys, Marlene Kelleher, Al Kline, Morag Maclachlan, Marion Mussell, Mabel Nichols, Mabel Pennier, Joanne Peterson, Laura Purcell, Lyn Ross, Rita Walsh, and George and Christie Wong. I thank each and every one of you for your generosity of spirit.

Irene was a proud supporter of scholarships established by the University of the Fraser Valley, earlier the University College of the Fraser Valley. I am mindful of the board minutes of February 3, 1999, noting how "Miss Irene Kelleher, at 96 years of age still a strong UCFV supporter, came by both to meet the new president and drop off a cheque for $4,000 to be added to the Mathilda and Cornelius Kelleher scholarship fund."[1]

All the royalties from *Invisible Generations* will go in her name to sustain the Julia Mathilda and Cornelius Kelleher Endowment Memorial Scholarship and the Irene Kelleher Memorial Endowment Bursary at the University of the Fraser Valley.

IRENE'S STORY

Invisible Generations tells Irene Kelleher's story.[2] Referring to herself and to her parents and grandparents, she admonished me time and again in our many conversations: "You have to tell what we told you."[3]

A much used maxim sums up attitudes within families like Irene's, of mixed Indigenous and white descent, who have lived in the Fraser Valley for generations. "You did not deny your heritage in your family, but you did not talk about it." In another version, "Grandmother always said don't deny your heritage, but don't give it freely." Within this frame of reference, today's Métis organizations targeting persons of mixed Indigenous and non-Indigenous descent are irrelevant. "I don't need an external source of identity—it's in my family."[4] Irene shared with me what she wanted to be told, and I do so here.

ORIGINS

Irene's story has its origin in time Irene and I spent together in the 1990s, during which she talked at length about her life experiences, and those of her parents and grandparents, in the Fraser Valley and also elsewhere in British Columbia. Lying to the east of the province's principal city of Vancouver, the Fraser Valley has been from time immemorial, and is today, home to diverse Indigenous peoples. Extensive non-Indigenous settlement goes back in time to the gold rush that occurred there in the mid-nineteenth century, with some earlier contact ensuing from a trade in animal pelts. By virtue of combining "white," to use the language of

the day and still used to describe persons with pale skin, and Indigenous descent, Irene and her family were long deemed to be beyond the
bounds of acceptability by the dominant white society. To be mixed was
not to belong.

Attracted to the future British Columbia by the gold rush, Irene's
white grandfathers partnered with Indigenous women. Mortimer Kelleher did so with Madeleine, whose father was from Nooksack in today's
Washington State, her mother from Matsqui in the Fraser Valley; Irene's
maternal grandfather, Joshua Wells, with Ki-ka-twa or Julia, born at Port
Douglas, situated along an early route to the goldfields.

Irene's parents wed on January 11, 1898, at St. Mary's Catholic
Mission, located on the north side of the Fraser River twelve kilometres
from today's Abbotsford. Oblate priest E.C. Chirouse joined together
Cornelius Kelleher, aged twenty-five years, with Julia Mathilda Wells,
who was twenty-one.[5] According to Irene, as the story was passed down
to her, "they had a wedding breakfast at the Wells home in Hatzic and
took the CPR train to Seattle and had a room at Fry's Hotel where they
saw prospectors readying to go to the Klondike gold rush."[6] Cornelius
recalled this critical event in his life:

> Sure enough, we were fortunate to get the room in the
> hotel because men were sleeping in the hallways of that
> hotel that night, waiting for the boat that would take them
> to Alaska and the goldfields. Seattle was a sight; every
> gadget under the sun was advertised on the street, men
> training [sled] dogs, and dogs selling as high as $150 and
> $200 apiece... the Alaska boat was loaded down and refus-
> ing passengers.[7]

Cornie and Mattie, as they were known, returned home by boat via Bellingham, where they stopped off to go to the theatre.[8]

A century and a quarter later, the stories of families like Irene's
living between Indigenous and white in the Fraser Valley, and across

British Columbia and Canada, still matter. The earliest newcomers to do so are remembered in the Fraser Valley by the impressive historic site that is Fort Langley, constructed in the 1820s by men in the employ of the fur-trading Hudson's Bay Company. There whites, part-Indigenous men, and some Indigenous Hawaiians formed families with local Indigenous women.[9] The gold rush of Irene's grandfathers in the mid-nineteenth century added a larger layer of newcomer men who partnered with Indigenous women. This aspect of our history has increasingly disappeared from view, due in part to Indigenous peoples and non-Indigenous arrivals each understandably highlighting their own stories.[10] To the extent that families that originated with a white forefather and an Indigenous foremother are still visible, it can sometimes seem contradictory, with white forefathers' surnames attached to the outwardly Indigenous persons who are their descendants.[11]

IRENE'S STORY

As are all our stories, Irene's story is not just any story. In the telling, Irene repeatedly referred to "my kind" and "our kind" to describe families like her own, living between Indigenous and white.[12] While not wholly Indigenous, their Indigenous descent set them apart from a white society that equated pale skin tones with moral superiority. The class of persons to which Irene and her family and their friends were relegated by whites was long known pejoratively as "half-breed," a term intentionally demeaning and stereotyping. For all that notions of "race," whereby physical features became social classifiers, have over time been discredited, the underlying assumptions long ruled supreme. To be white conferred an inherent right, so white people thought, not only to be in charge but also to set the boundaries of inclusion and thereby the exclusion of others. As recently summed up by a scholar of the subject, whiteness, "largely a social construction shaped, defined, and contested by those claiming whiteness and those arbitrating it," became "the standard by which others were to be judged" and found wanting.[13] Wholly

Indigenous persons were early on legislated out of existence in British Columbia and across North America, being relegated to reserves or reservations and only recently, through their own efforts, acquiring a modicum of respectability. Much the same inequitable treatment occurred in Canada respecting Indigenous women who dared to marry non-Indigenous men: along with their descendants, they were legally dispossessed as Indigenous persons.

Those who, like Irene and her family and friends, embodied both Indigenous and white descent counted for naught, their stories without meaning. "We were second-class citizens. There's nobody to write about us; it will be the first time to tell the story," Irene explained to me not long after we met at the suggestion of a mutual acquaintance.[14]

Irene not only wanted her family's story told, but also knew how she wanted it told, and I was a willing listener. From Irene's perspective I was, I suspect, the best possible intermediary to do so on her terms. I was aware from my first visit that Irene used the "we" in our conversations "always in reference to Native people." I noted to myself at the time how "she lives and has lived in a largely white world but inside is an Indian woman."[15] My teaching in the Faculty of Education at the University of British Columbia, where Irene had studied and where I worked with Indigenous students, made me, I came to realize, a trustworthy conduit. I would respect her for her life course and her teaching career rather than looking down on her as lesser than myself.[16]

I liked Irene. I enjoyed her company. Not only was our time together a welcome respite from the everyday life of UBC, but each time we talked I learned a lot from a new perspective about the ways of the world, and of the Fraser Valley. At that point in time I sat on a provincial board, BC Heritage Trust, which took us around the province for meetings with local folk, but in an us-and-them fashion. We came, we saw, we listened, we took note of initiatives, and we left before most conversations had time to reach a satisfactory conclusion. I had recently published a history of British Columbia, which similarly made me realize how unfinished was my understanding of the province I called home.[17]

Living all her life between Indigenous and white by virtue of her descent, retired school-teacher Irene Kelleher was adamant that invisible generations like hers should no longer be hidden from view. *Wigwams to Windmills*, 117

Irene's project became a joint activity. "You have to tell what we told you," the plural "we" referring both to her parents and grandparents and to trusted others she told me about or took me to visit.[18] Irene shared copies of her own writing and transcripts of interviews by others of her or her parents, which we would have photocopied for me to take away to integrate into an emerging text. My confidence in the project grew on overhearing Irene tell a friend who phoned while I was visiting that "there's a teacher here from the UBC and she's interviewing me and... she's going to be on our side... *I know that* [Irene's emphases]."[19] During our conversations, Irene was very much in charge of the telling. "I've got to get the Kelleher story down" was her repeated refrain. I jotted a memo to myself following an early visit: "Irene moves quickly—she darts—and she thinks just as quickly—her mind darts."[20] I scrambled to keep up.

As Irene many times reminded me, it was not only herself but also her parents who wanted the family's story told, as indicated by their writing and interviews. They were the pivots to Irene's long life. She admired their characters and resourcefulness, and most of all their determination to make good lives in sometimes adverse circumstances. Her parents withstood, much as she did herself as a career schoolteacher, attitudes in the larger society that diminished persons like them, based solely on their genetic inheritance. It is the combination of these factors that gave Irene's story its resonance for me. Irene's story is about hard-working, everyday people, as most of us are, perforce leading extraordinary lives.

Whereas Irene's life crossed the twentieth century, her parents and grandparents linked her into the century before. Irene's white grandfathers were born in the 1820s, her Indigenous grandmothers about 1845 to 1850. Born in 1872 and 1876, Irene's father and mother died in 1969 and 1967 respectively. Her parents repeatedly shared their life experiences and those of their own parents with, among others, Imbert Orchard of the Canadian Broadcasting Corporation. Irene recalled how "Imbert Orchard came up more than once. He'd meet me at the school [where she then taught] and drive me up to the homestead [where her parents lived] and would have supper with Mom and Dad."[21]

OUR TIME TOGETHER

Irene guided our time together. Following the Imbert Orchard model, but at a different time of the day, I would be invited for early morning coffee. After coffee, we talked, and then might drive to lunch, possibly at Irene's favourite restaurant, followed by several stops for errands on the way back to her Abbotsford condominium. Other times, at Irene's suggestion, we drove the Fraser Valley of her grandparents, parents, and herself, to locations she brought to life as she knew them so that I might do so as well.

Once our relationship fell into place, my scholarly self sounded an alert. I should tape-record our exchanges in the interest of reliability and authenticity. Transcribed professionally by a third party, the result of our first taped conversation annoyed Irene, whose own tape recorder she considered "such a nuisance."[22]

> Irene: Well, that's good.
>
> Jean: That's good coffee. It's hot.
>
> Irene: Well, I know something for sure. I've got to get the Kelleher story down.
>
> Jean: Yes. That's absolutely true.

Neither of us liked what we read. Given, almost inevitably, the transcribed social trivia and hesitations that were intertwined with what we were about, Irene insisted, and I agreed, that the best course was for me to take what I described to Irene as inconspicuous "off and on notes on our conversations," transcribe them as soon as I got home an hour's drive away, and pass them on to Irene the next time we met for her consideration and editing.[23]

Between our visits, there might be phone calls from Irene critiquing and elaborating on what I had written either in my notes or in a composite text that was slowly emerging. She sometimes lamented what she did not know and asked me to find out more from written or manuscript sources to which I had access to pass on to her the next time we met.

Insights from these sources might then find their way into and comple-
ment her story.

Gradually, a narrative emerged that went through various iterations, until one day half a dozen years after we first met, Irene was satis-
fied with the current version. I had taken to heart her self-reflection that
"only she could write the intimate details," and been as honest as I could
about what she shared during our conversations.[24] Irene phoned full of
enthusiasm. "I burned the midnight oil. I read every word of it. I wouldn't
change a word of it, except for when I was born, on the 16th [the result of
a typo]. When I read it through, I had nothing to correct. Where did you
get all that information?"[25]

I sent Irene a clean version, which I followed up with one of our
usual visits. After morning coffee and a snack, at her suggestion we went
to the Mission Museum. As we walked around, we chatted about this and
that. Filling in some details, Irene explained that when Imbert Orchard
interviewed her parents in 1963 they still used coal lamps. She mused:
"Oh, Uncle Andrew could play the violin!" Talking about herself in the
third person, she shared once again how "she wasn't accepted."[26]

While we continued to see each other from time to time and we
remained friends, we had completed the essence of our task together.
Irene died on March 16, 2004, having the previous December 16 celebrated her 102nd birthday with a large party at the care home where
she was then living.[27]

SITUATING IRENE'S STORY

For all of its particulars, Irene's story is not unique. The mixture of Indigenous and white descent that marked Irene, her family, and friends was
not exclusively theirs, but was shared during those years and into the
present day by many others across the Fraser Valley, British Columbia,
Canada, and the world. Whatever the location, individuals and families
similarly experienced differential treatment they had no capacity to
fully remedy except to deny who they were in the interests of fitting into
a prejudiced larger society. Only rarely, as with the Métis of Red River

in today's Manitoba and west into Saskatchewan and with Mestizos in Mexico and Peru, have persons of mixed Indigenous and white descent redefined themselves as counterpoints to the dominant society.

Irene and her family chose not to deny who they were, but rather stood tall and bore the consequences. Irene's references to "our kind" and to "second-class citizens" were not made lightly, but reflected a long life lived well, but not necessarily easily. For Irene, as for her parents, the burden of mixed descent, of being a "half-breed," was ever present. It was able to be put on hold in the moment by socializing with, and caring for, others of similar backgrounds, only to return unexpectedly and very possibly in double measure.

Irene's life crossed three generations of her family in British Columbia's Fraser Valley. While her grandfathers died before she was born, she met both her Indigenous grandmothers. Irene was taken to visit her maternal Wells grandmother when she was ill and dying, and she remembered her paternal Kelleher grandmother coming to see them but could not, to her regret, recall about either of them "what they talked like." Referencing one and then the other, "I hardly knew her." [28] With Irene's passing, these three generations of shared memories are no longer part of lived experience.

On Irene's death in 2004, I put her story aside. My concern not to intrude on her memory vied with her instructions to me that the story be told. Having over the years shared echoes of it with others, I became increasingly aware that Irene's story has meaning beyond particular individuals and locales. As well as speaking to all those who have lived, and still live, between Indigenous and white, Irene's story is part of our common history as British Columbians, Canadians, and human beings.

Dear Irene, this is your story as you wanted it told.

IRENE'S PATERNAL INHERITANCE

Irene's story as she shared it with me always began with her parents and before them her grandparents. All her life she felt herself embedded in their lives and they in hers. She was ever conscious that except for them she would have, in a literal sense, not existed—much less have had the determination to live as she would, to the extent she did, for a century and more.

Neither of Irene's parents, Cornelius Kelleher and Julia Mathilda Wells, had usual childhoods, any more than did most of the contemporaries who became their lifelong friends, or as their daughter, Irene, did. Most fathers were gold miners come to get rich quick who had tarried and begot families with Indigenous women. Both Cornie's and Mattie's mothers left their families when their children were still very young, whereas for others, it was fathers who disappeared from view. For Cornie, the school run by the Oblate religious order at St. Mary's Mission where he and Mattie wed provided his fundamental formative experience.[29] The stability of Irene's parents' marriage over almost seventy years demonstrates the capacity of individuals who were determined to lead their lives on their own terms, whatever the circumstances of their upbringing had been.

Irene's father, Cornelius Kelleher, was born in 1872. His parents were an Irishman named Mortimer Kelleher and a Nooksack woman her son named at his own marriage as Magdelan Triloures.[30] Irene recalled her paternal grandmother as Madeleine Job.[31] Most of what we know about Mortimer Kelleher and the Nooksack woman with whom he partnered was passed down to their son and granddaughter.

Irene's paternal grandfather, Mortimer Kelleher, had been in British Columbia a dozen or more years by the time his son was born in 1872. While Mortimer's story is unique to him, as are all our stories to ourselves, it is also representative of generations of newcomers who, for one reason or another, left the set of circumstances into which they had been born for another set, whose outcome they could not possibly have foreseen at the time they headed out.

CHARMED BY GOLD

Mortimer Kelleher was the eldest of three sons of a draper, or cloth merchant, in Macroom, County Cork, Ireland. His son, Cornelius, recounted his father's story as it came down to him:

> My dad left Ireland when he was quite young. His dad wanted him to marry a rich, moneyed woman. He wouldn't listen to that, so he ran away to sea. He came to San Francisco, got off there—jumped ship—ran away from the ship. He was going to go to the goldfields. That kind of petered out. Then there was a big Indian uprising there in the Yakimas, so he enlisted into the American army to fight the Indians.[32]

Mortimer had been caught up by the mighty California gold rush that began in 1848, along with many thousands of men from around the world. Not as successful there as they had hoped, most men who were not returning home soon headed off to the next reported finds, which included the homeland of the Yakima people along the Yakima River in today's south-central Washington State, where gold was discovered in 1855. The Yakimas were at this point in time being coerced onto a reservation to make way for newcomer settlement and now found even their greatly reduced territory overrun by outsiders. They protested, and the

United States Army, having none of it, sent in troops, whose ranks were enhanced by volunteers such as young Kelleher. It was as an offshoot of the expanding hostilities that troops were dispatched in late 1856 to protect white settlers around Bellingham Bay in American territory, which may account for his having been discharged there.

Still smitten with gold, Mortimer Kelleher walked from Whatcom, renamed Bellingham, to Fort Langley.[33] Gold discoveries on the nearby Fraser River in 1858 attracted many thousands of miners from California and elsewhere. Most of them headed up the coast by water and landed in Victoria, then the capital of the British colony of Vancouver Island. From there, they made their way across the Strait of Georgia to the new gold strikes. So many miners did so that, by the end of 1858, the British government had created a second British colony of British Columbia. The new colony encompassed the mainland territory that had been acquired, along with the earlier colony of Vancouver Island, when the Pacific Northwest was divided between Britain and the United States in 1846. American entrepreneurs south of the new international border were not to be circumvented. Seeking to persuade California miners heading north to land at Whatcom Bay and buy their provisions there, rather than in Victoria, they constructed an overland trail to Fort Langley, which must have been the route Mortimer took. The trail was extremely arduous and soon fell into disuse (although it is still marked in the present day), but it clearly suited Irene's grandfather.

As had been the case since the California rush of 1848, new gold finds were ever farther north. By the early 1860s, they were being reported in the Cariboo region of today's central British Columbia, and it was there Mortimer headed next. According to his son's narrative: "He worked there for quite a while."[34]

SETTLING DOWN

By the mid-1860s, Mortimer Kelleher had had enough of gold mining. He decided, like most of his contemporaries who remained in British Columbia—a minority of the miners, most of whom moved on—to take up land. From 1860 onwards, any British male or other male new-comer who swore allegiance to the British Crown could go anywhere except for a townsite or Indigenous settlement and stake up to 160 acres. This pre-empted land could, on demonstrating certain improve-ments, be permanently acquired as a Crown grant. The fertile Fraser Valley was particularly desirable, and it was there Mortimer headed. On February 18, 1864, he pre-empted 160 acres of land on the south side of the Fraser River.[35]

The next step for many newcomer men in similar circumstances was to find a woman with whom to share the hard work that followed the acquisition of land. The task was complicated by the fact that the fur trade and then the gold rush were almost wholly male adventures in what was the most distant corner of North America, without easy links to the larger world. At the time of the earliest count, in 1870, three out of every four non-Indigenous adults living in British Columbia, which by then occupied the same area as the present-day province, were men. Mortimer Kelleher was not alone in turning to an Indigenous woman.

Having met her on his earlier travels, Mortimer formed an attach-ment to Madeleine, whose parents, Job and Mary, according to their grandson Cornelius, "had a homestead" on traditional Nooksack land in American territory about thirty kilometres south of Mortimer's holding.[36] Mary was originally from Matsqui, just north of the international border, and had married Job at Nooksack.[37] Mortimer's prospective in-laws were not opposed to Madeleine's union with a white man since Job's sister had wed a newcomer man herself.[38] Like many of their contemporar-ies, the family criss-crossed categories put into place by whites and also a border that similarly held little or no meaning to them. According to their son, Cornelius, Mortimer and Madeleine "were married in 1867, in Nooksack, by Father Paul Durieu," an Oblate priest.[39]

The Kellehers left the original pre-emption and relocated north of the Fraser River two years later, due to seasonal flooding.[40] As their son later explained: "The water kept coming up every year so he quit that and came over to this side of the river—the Mission side of the river—

and he took up that ranch where Mission City is now."[41] On November 30, 1869, Mortimer pre-empted 160 acres "situated about ¾ kilometre below the Catholic St. Mary's Mission, established eight years earlier on the north bank of the Fraser River."[42] According to Cornelius, his parents built a log cabin, "cleaned it up and planted potatoes and vegetables and caught fish in the river, and meat in the woods."[43] Self-sufficiency was the order of the day.

Nearby St. Mary's Mission, run by the Missionary Oblates of Mary Immaculate (OMI), made it possible, Cornie explained, for his father to earn that little bit of cash essential to survival.

> He worked for the OMI mission, for a few dollars. Pretty near all these old ranchers and a lot more of them who went to the Cariboo and couldn't get much gold and got broken, well, they'd come down here. They had ranches around. They got work from the mission. That's how they [the priests] got their grist mill and sawmill going, with these fellows.[44]

Mortimer Kelleher walked to the mission every day the weather was fit to work.

PARENTHOOD

Two children were born to Mortimer and Madeleine, a son, Cornelius, on April 22, 1872, and a daughter, Mary Theresa, two years later.[45] Indigenous and newcomer practices interacted in the birth of their eldest child. Irene wrote in one of her publications: "A few weeks before he was born, his mother, who wanted to be with her people when her child was born, walked from Mission, over to her people's tribe near Nooksack, Washington." As to how she managed the thirty-kilometre trek, according to her son: "She followed the trail used by the Indians when going to Nooksack.... Then on the ninth day I must be christened in the Catholic Church at St. Mary's Mission, so she carried me back."[46]

Irene's grandparents, Irishman Mortimer Kelleher, captivated by a gold rush beginning in British Columbia in 1858, and a Nooksack woman named Madeleine, chose as godfather to their son, Cornelius, born in 1872, their Fraser Valley neighbour Joseph Deroche, seated second from right on his porch. Mission Community Archives, 198302-3554

Cornelius's godparents at his baptism were Joseph and Marie Deroche, who lived about sixteen kilometres east of the mission and were, in their sturdy character, very like the Kellehers. Joe's parents were so ordinary that, born in the mid-1830s in Montreal, he did not learn to read or write but, according to his daughter, signed with an "X."[47] Joe left home when he was seventeen and worked in New York and Milwaukee before heading to the California gold rush in 1852 and, a decade later, north to the Cariboo.[48] He soon decided that greater riches were to be had as a teamster, driving goods by wagon and oxen to and from the goldfields.[49] It was the search for a place to winter his oxen that drew Joe to the meadowlands of Nicomen Island, cut off from the Fraser River by a narrow stretch of water known as Nicomen Slough. The gold rush's decline may have prompted him to pre-empt 160 acres there in 1868 and so become that area's first non-Indigenous settler.[50] As was the practice at the time, Joe built himself a log cabin, planted a garden and perhaps an orchard, acquired some domestic animals, "paddled down

Just as Montrealer Joe Deroche was Cornelius Kelleher's godfather, his godmother was Joe's wife, Marie, daughter of a French-Canadian fur trade labourer at nearby Fort Langley and a Kwakiutl or Kwakwaka'wakw woman from Vancouver Island. Mission Community Archives, MCA 219-09

Everyday life for early newcomers to the Fraser Valley comes through in this image with Joe Deroche seated on the far left of the wagon. Mission Community Archives, MCA-0116-S025-002

to New Westminster for his first tea, flour, and sugar," and, so far as was possible, sought self-sufficiency.[51]

The Marie who became Joe Deroche's wife and Cornelius's god-mother was the daughter of a French-Canadian fur trade labourer, Antoine Danneau, who had arrived in the Pacific Northwest in 1849 and was eventually stationed at Fort Langley, and of a Kwakiutl, or Kwakwa-ka'wakw, woman from coastal British Columbia.[52] When she died, Danneau took his motherless daughter, Marie, to the school for girls operated at St. Mary's Mission by the Sisters of St. Ann, who had arrived in British Columbia from Quebec at the beginning of the gold rush. There Marie in due course encountered the much older Deroche. At the time of their marriage in 1874, she was eighteen and Joe Deroche was approaching forty, a not unusual age difference among gold miners settling down with local women.[53] In retrospect, Mortimer Kelleher chose his son's godparents well, giving his infant son a bulwark in a world that would soon crumble down around him.

FAMILY DISRUPTION

When Cornelius Kelleher was just seven and his sister, Maria Theresa, five, life as they knew it came to an abrupt end. "The people in the early days used to call me Mort's boy, when I was a little fellow. The neighbours, you know." Cornie would no longer be Mort's boy, at least not literally so.[54] "My father took pneumonia, and the priests took him to New Westminster [the nearest location with a hospital], and he died there in July 1879."[55]

The pneumonia to which Mortimer succumbed may have been the effect rather than the cause of the family breakup. Cornie once shared with Irene that "Mortimer told Madeleine that he was going to take the son back to Ireland and she beat him up."[56] In this version of events, Madeleine escaped with her two children home to Nooksack, but somehow the priests intruded. They not only confiscated the children, but quickly married Madeleine off to another man, likely to ensure that she did not steal them away again.[57] The Oblate records attest that on September 16, 1880, "Magdeline widow of Mortimer Kelher of St. Mary" wed "George chief of Matsqui" in a Catholic ceremony at the mission.[58]

The Oblates retained custody of the two children, even though, as Cornelius was led to believe, according to Irene, "his Grandparents Kelleher from Ireland had wanted him in their custody." Two reasons suggest themselves as to why young Cornelius remained in BC. The first has to do with Mortimer Kelleher's large landholding adjacent to the mission. As Irene put it with more than a little irony: "The OMI having custody of Cornelius and Mary Theresa, also had custody of Mortimer's property."[59] Provincial government records attest that the pre-emption of 160 acres was still in the name of the deceased "Mort. C. Kelleher" at the time it became a Crown grant on January 21, 1885, five years after his death. The property would eventually be subdivided as the town of Mission.[60]

The second reason the Oblates may have held on to Cornelius and Mary Theresa was equally self-centred. The order's rationale for being in the Fraser Valley, and having itself pre-empted 160 acres of land in 1862, was to establish a boarding school for the children of the Indigenous peoples they had come to convert to Catholicism.[61] A boys' school opened in 1863; an adjacent counterpart for girls run by the Sisters of St. Ann began in 1868. From 1874 onwards, the schools received an annual Canadian government grant of $350, raised to $500 in 1883, for the purpose of educating Indigenous children.[62]

The catch was that Indigenous peoples did not necessarily agree with the Oblates' plan for them, while the Catholics needed warm bodies to fill the spaces. [63] So the Oblates compromised and then prevaricated with the tacit consent of government officials. The boys' school was acknowledged as of 1875–76 to be enrolling a mix of "native and half breed boys," the account referencing "the camps, or lodges of absolutely uncivilized natives, ignorant, uncouth" whence they came.[64] In 1881, British Columbia Indian Commissioner I.W. Powell reported that "about 20 pupils attend there but I believe they are half-breeds."[65] Seven years later, he acknowledged privately that "at present most of the attendees are half breeds."[66] Within this context, the Kelleher siblings were quite simply too good to pass up.

To ensure the desired outcome, events were arranged so that the two youngsters' mother was otherwise occupied. Not only was Madeleine married off, her new husband may have been rewarded for doing so. According to her son, "the priests made George chief of Matsqui Reserve.... George Matsqui was the first chief appointed by the priests."[67] Also keeping Madeleine busy were the couple's three young children.[68]

So, according to Irene, her father and aunt effectively belonged to the Oblates. As she put it to me: "Mrs. Kelleher was directed by the OMI priests to have Cornelius and his little sister placed in the OMI boarding school to be raised."[69] Cornie reiterated the point: "Bishop d'Herbomez, Bishop of New Westminster, took over the property, and he and Brother Rine were my guardians. After the Bishop's death, Bishop Durieu was my guardian."[70]

Young Cornelius Kelleher's life soon became even lonelier. He and his sister spent their first two years at St. Mary's together, even though they were isolated from each other. Another student during the same years described how a tight and high board fence separated the boys'

Following an argument, possibly over Mortimer Kelleher wanting to take their two children to Ireland, Irene's maternal grandmother, Madeleine, escaped with them to Nooksack, only to have the Oblates confiscate the children, send them to St. Mary's Mission school, and marry her off to a Matsqui said to have been appointed chief of the local reserve as a reward for marrying her. Madeleine is pictured here with her second family. Mission Community Archives, MCA-0228-0021-000

section of the school run by the Oblates from the girls' section under the charge of the Sisters of St. Ann.[71]

Then Maria Theresa Kelleher died. As recalled by Cornelius: "She didn't live very long after she came to the convent. She was about seven when she came and she took cold, and there were no medicines and she died."[72] She was "buried at the OMI cemetery."[73] After that, perhaps due to her daughter's death, Cornelius's mother, Madeleine, did not visit often, Irene recalled being told by her father.[74]

EVERYDAY LIFE FOR BOYS AT ST. MARY'S MISSION SCHOOL

St. Mary's Mission became Cornelius Kelleher's home and also his family. While it is impossible to reconstruct everyone young Cornie got to know among the other boys, the twenty-odd pupils enumerated in the 1881 Canadian census had, like him, white fathers and almost certainly Indigenous mothers.[75]

Mary's Mission school had separate residences for male and female students; this photograph of the girls' residence shows the uniformity of their dress. Mission Community Archives, MCA-060-11A

Among Cornie's fellow students were the Baker brothers, Alonzo and Joseph, who, although five and three years Cornie's senior, became lifelong friends. Their father, Ferdinand Boulanger, had left Quebec in 1849 to work his way on a sailing vessel to the California gold rush. On the way, he changed his name to Peter Baker to avoid detection when he jumped ship at the site of the future Panama Canal. Walking across the isthmus, he managed to board a ship going to California. Later, following in Mortimer Kelleher's footsteps, he went north to the goldfields in present-day British Columbia.[76] In the spring of 1863, Peter Baker pre-empted 160 acres "on the north bank of the Fraser River opposite to Fort Langley," and settled down with Mary Brousseau. Her father, Basil, had come west from Montreal in 1833 to work at Fort Langley, and her mother was a Kwantlen woman named Rose.[77] The Bakers raised a large family.[78]

Many of Cornelius Kelleher's fellow students at St. Mary's shared the common bond of being dispatched there on a parent's death. Among them was Colfax Cunningham, three years older than Cornie, whose "father was killed in a mill accident" when "one winter he slipped and fell on a circular saw."[79]

Other fathers had simply disappeared, or so it seemed with "Bloody" Edwards, remembered by a daughter-in-law as "Blondel Edwards, Queen's Navy officer, a Welsh man, this is all I know of his family."[80] Nick-named "Bloody" for his colourful language, Edwards reportedly "came out here as a sailor" and then, according to a long-time Mission resident, panned for gold.[81] A fellow miner recalled an encounter with him at the celebration of Queen Victoria's birthday on May 24, 1859, at Yale, located a hundred kilometres northeast of Mission.

> The bulk of the crowd were Yankees and they were cheeky to[o]—but Edwards did not care for that he should and hollar Queen Victoria forever and at last the Yankees dip him in the rincar and soon as he got out of the water he holarred again to the top of vois Queen for ever. An old Yankee shouted to the fellow that was putting Edwards in the river to leave the man alone he was the bravest little man I ever saw... this man walk to the edge of the river and took Edwards by the hand and led him to a Sloon with the crowd follow him and cheering Bloody Edwards and those who dip him in the river did pack him on their shoulders from Sloon to Sloon all day he was the biggest man in Yale that day.[82]

Bloody Edwards lived for a time in Hope, where he had three children by one or more Indigenous women between about 1860 and 1864.[83] His son Patrick described his mother at his marriage as "Cather-ine Indian woman," his siblings, Henry and Mary, on their marriages as "Siama, Indian woman."[84]

Patrick, Mary Ellen, and Henry Edwards recalled speaking "Indian" as their first language, which suggests they lived for a time within a mater-nal setting.[85] Indicative of the children's in-between status, Henry would later act as a court interpreter for Indigenous persons.[86] The family story is that Edwards returned to Wales but, before doing so, bequeathed his land to the Oblates in exchange for bringing up his three children.[87]

Also among this generation of fatherless boys—some of whom likely became stand-ins for the older brothers Cornie did not have or the father he had lost—was Charles Gardner, born in 1860 and so a dozen years Cornie's senior. Charlie's mother was Selaamia, described as the daughter of the chief of Matsqui and Sumas and granddaughter of See-am, once chief from Yale to the mouth of the Fraser. Charlie's father, Charles Clinton Gardner, had studied at Columbia University in New York City and was a United States army lieutenant. At the time of his son's birth, Gardner headed a boundary commission surveying the border between the United States and British territory, and for a time had charge of an astronomical station on Chilliwack Lake, located southeast of today's city of the same name.[88]

Charlie Gardner never met his father, who arranged through intermediaries for him to be protected, and for him and Selaamia to be given supplies on a regular basis. This practice continued until Selaamia was informed that four-year-old Charles was to be sent away to school in Victoria on faraway Vancouver Island, whereupon she reported back that he had died. Charlie was thereupon raised by her as an Indigenous child until the priests at the mission persuaded Selaamia to let her then ten-year-old also learn newcomer ways.[89] In old age, he recalled his mother telling him, "You have learned all that my people have to teach you, Charlie, now you must go to learn from your father's people."[90] By the time Cornelius arrived at St. Mary's Mission in 1879, Charles Gardner was a senior boy, in charge of the daily bread-making, among other responsibilities.

The reason Cornelius Kelleher and his classmates were at the mission was to become literate as well as to become good Catholics. As explained by Irene, "Cornelius stayed... for approximately ten years, during which time he was educated."[91] Cornie recalled about his schooling:

> My first school teacher was a German that was Captain
> Henry. He was supposed to be a captain on a sailing boat.
> He got off of it to go to the gold fields, and didn't make it.
> So he came back down here and he joined the [Mission]

and taught school... and boy, when I couldn't go up to the blackboard, boy, he'd hit you on the fingers with a rod.... We had mostly French teachers trying to teach us English.... Most all them priests that were here were French or Belgians.[92]

Irene, who would make her career as a schoolteacher, considered that her father's "hand writing is very legible and the spelling 'good'—a credit to his OMI teachers."[93] Throughout his life, Cornelius would keep a diary. His entries centred on weather and visitors and showed an appreciation of opportunities to read new books.[94] He was grateful to an early neighbour: "He had a log house, and he used to have books right up to the ceiling. I used to, when I first came over on the prairie, I used to jump on the horse and go over there and get a book. 'Take this one,' he'd say, 'this is good.'"[95]

Living conditions at the mission were simple. As described by Cornelius, originally "there were log buildings, not very elaborate things either, but after they go sawing lumber, they built better ones." During the winter: "Oh, boy, it was cold, you know, when the winds would blow, I'll tell you. You know, them rough boards—no planing mills in them days, you know."[96]

All the same, these were children, and so there were also "all kinds of tricks," such as night-time pillow fights and insistence on washing in the creek even when there was a layer of ice on top of the water. The natural environment functioned as a playground.

> We used to get in the water and swim across the [Fraser] river, you know, and backwards again. We thought nothing of it. We'd just get in and swim over the river, and sometimes we'd drift quite a piece down, we'd walk up the bank and come right back over to the other side again. Quite a few of the boys, you know, young fellows like myself, we'd jump in and swim across the river and come back again.[97]

Cornelius did a lot of hard physical labour while at the mission school: "they had to support themselves, you see."[98] The religious order operated a farm on the opposite, Matsqui, side of the Fraser River and a grist mill near the river. Fields were ploughed by oxen and harvesting done with hand sickles, threshing with a long pole stretched across a length of canvas. The smaller boys beat the kernels out with sticks, the larger ones with flails. "It was surprising how much wheat we would thresh in one day this way."[99] Like many of the others, Cornie took his turn working in the grist mill. "I was filling flour sacks, and middlings and shorts and bran and so on, and weighing it."[100]

The seasonal round also had the boys crossing the river to Matsqui to mow the hay grown there.[101] "A lot of hay was cut by a lot of boys in a few days."[102] Cornie recalled how "when it got too hot we'd go down and jump in the river and swim around, and then go back cutting hay."[103] The most pleasurable aspect was that the boys got to sleep in the newly mown hay and in the morning to cook their own breakfasts before having to stack the hay and get it into a large storage barn that stood on the bank of the river.[104] "We cut hay there every fall after the water went down [in the river] and then hauled it there. Then we would haul it to the Mission side on a big scow."[105]

Cornelius did not work only on the farm. As he shared with his daughter, Irene, "one of the jobs he had as a student was assisting... in operating the St. Mary's Mission Water Power Flour Mill. There he ground wheat, corn & peas."[106] Cornie took pride in how "the wheat that we grew was all ground, we had our own mill."[107] The school also had a lumber mill. He worked there as a "sawmill pusher" and, when older, helped to cut and haul logs to the mill. During his time at the mission, enough lumber was harvested to build a church and two log buildings on each side of it, one to house the boys and one the girls who were being schooled there.[108]

As Indian residential schools across Canada did, the mission produced its own food, which meant pigs, sheep, and cattle to be raised, killed, and salted, and potatoes and peas to be grown.[109] "We sheared the sheep when we got quite a few of them, and then we had a carting mill that came from somewhere, France possibly.... We grew a lot of peas, for pea soup. And the pigs, we slaughtered them in the fall here, for our food."[110] As well, "there was an orchard there... there were fruit trees there of all description. Apple trees and graphs [grafts] that he [Father Foquet] had brought from Oregon and France."[111] Cornie remembered Indigenous people coming down the river with canoes filled with salmon that had been smoked at the school.[112]

> And we had the canoes, we would set our lines, and catch sturgeon, great big ones—100 pounders. That would be cut up and salted, and some of it dried. We never went hungry. We had rough stuff. No sweet cakes, or anything else. I remember when I first went there, the only time we had any sweet stuff was at Christmas, and that was black strap molasses, see, put onto the bread, and some of it we got to lick up on our plates.

Cattle were raised for food, so "we never had milk for years and years, though we had cattle there."[113] Food preparation was immediate and direct.

> Just an open fireplace. Boil it, as you say—pea soup and boiled beef and boiled salmon and roast salmon and so on. You boiled.... They had great big brass kettles, that they used to make the soup and boil the meat and potatoes and vegetables in. They hung over the fireplace and everything was cooked in there.... They were monstrous big things. They hung over the fireplace—this stone fireplace, where they cooked their stuff.... They used to haul the big logs in with the ox teams. In the wintertime we'd saw them by the cross-cut saws, and so on, and split them up.[114]

Growing Up between Indigenous and White

The full extent to which Cornelius Kelleher was caught between Indigenous and white, rather than considering himself one or the other, is apparent in his ambivalent response to the Indigenous people who contributed to the life of St. Mary's Mission. "They always had lots of Indians and their families around. They built log cabins all along the banks of the river. They lived there and they helped the OMI priest wonderfully." He recalled how "back of the church was a row of houses where the Indians who were working for the mission used to live."[115] During his first year there, students were taken to visit the Sechelt people living northwest of today's Vancouver, and the next year the Sechelt people and others camped at the mission for similar activities.[116] The young Cornelius perceived these people to be distinct from himself: "I never saw so many tents and so many Indians, both Coast and river Indians were there in thousands."[117]

The aspect of the mission that was most intended to effect change among Indigenous peoples were Passion plays depicting the death of Jesus according to the New Testament. The performances engaged Cornelius's interest, but not in relation to himself. Irene "remembered her father telling stories, and describing the Passion plays at the local Mission during the celebrations of the church year."[118] Cornie also did so in an interview conducted with him in the early 1960s:

> The first I remember was in 1880. Indians came in canoes from as far away as Sechelt. As they neared their destination the canoes spread out, and the occupants, with great noise and singing as they rowed, thus announced their arrival. They brought with them tents and cooking utensils and supplies for camping. For the Play the actors were in full dress depicting the time of Christ. The celebration lasted for a week.[119]

He didn't perceive these arrivals or the play to be linked to himself:

> The first Passion play I saw was in 1880. They had their
> Passion play in the lower house down by the river. The
> procession had to go through our yard, in back of the
> Priests' house, and to the church. They had an altar at
> the end, made of cedar boughs and trees and another
> one in the yard at the other end. And the Bishop would
> carry the host from one to the other. He would deposit it
> at one place, and they'd all sit down and do their praying
> and singing. And then he'd pick that up and they'd move
> to the next one over by the creek. They had two altars. The
> Indian women would go into the bush and collect all the
> flower petals and leaves they could find and strew them in
> front of the Bishop as he walked.... They'd follow him with
> different songs. Different tribes had their own song and
> their own language.[120]

A second, more developed Passion play occurred in front of the main buildings, where the visiting Indigenous peoples hung Japanese lanterns between the trees.

> They would start from the foot of the hills there, doing
> their singing. And each tribe had so many candles that
> they lit in the evening. Everyone carried a lit candle as
> they went up singing. They would go to the shrine there
> and do a little song and prayer there and start back.[121]

A third Passion play, staged during the flood of 1894, was particularly noteworthy. "Indians coming from Squamish, Sechelt, Langley, Pt. Douglas, and Chilliwack... brought their bands with them and put on wonderful concerts."[122] In Cornelius's description:

> They had an image of Christ on the cross, and they trained
> these women, and had some men dressed as centurion
> soldiers. And one man carried a spear, and the women

dressed like the virgin Mary. They would kneel under the cross and this fellow would punch a hole in this plaster image, and this red ink would run down on these women. They would kneel right at the foot of the cross. The band would play and there was an old fella named Captain John, he used to have a cannon on the hillside, and he would yell out "fire" and bang she'd go. And then the bands would start to play. [123]

These later descriptions underline the deep impression the Passion plays had on a young Cornelius Kelleher and almost certainly on others as well. The extent to which they formed Cornie's identity as living between Indigenous and white is less clear.

The Coming of the Railway

While still at school, Cornelius was repeatedly made aware that the world of his childhood was slipping away. British Columbia was changing in some fundamental ways, bringing in growing numbers of newcomers with less sensitivity than their predecessors to Indigenous people and to those like himself of mixed descent.

One day in September 1882, railway surveyors arrived. "The men would tell us kids that after a while there would be a railway coming through. We hadn't the faintest idea what a railway looked like." That autumn, trees were felled along the right-of-way, and in the winter and summer, there were grading gangs. The day the first locomotive came chugging along, students were in a class, but "we poured out the doors and windows in a rush and our teachers couldn't stop us," and were given a ride to Hatzic about six kilometres away along the Fraser River. [124] These were formative experiences for a lifetime. "Pretty near all this whole gang was on there. We thought that was great." [125]

The rail line brought changes with it. The Canadian Pacific Railway had acquired the right-of-way along the river itself, forcing the school to move farther up the hill. [126] The right-of-way took away the apple orchard, and the mission relocated to where most of the junk and rubbish had been dumped, whose removal and the planting of a new orchard meant even more work for the boys at the school. Once trains began running, it was possible to bring in flour for baking bread rather than growing wheat. The railway also made it possible for the priests to acquire a hand printing press, and a prize of a five-quart bottle of molasses was announced to the boy learning to use it most accurately and rapidly, which Cornelius won. He was a staff favourite, recalling how a bishop who "was a great fisherman" would "always get me to go along with him" fishing.[127]

The railway also facilitated a new form of community, one that was common at Indian residential schools across British Columbia and beyond. That winter the boys at the school practised their band instruments particularly diligently, and the next summer, they were taken by rail to Yale in the Fraser Canyon. From there, they then walked to Lytton to give concerts to the railway gangs in order to raise money to buy an organ for the church.[128] "We had a real swell time with those camp men and they gave their money generously. At nights we would play our band and sing our songs outside in the open air. At quite a few of the camps the men would sing too."[129] The band proved a very effective means to promote the mission, so when, during these same years, the steamboat *Elizabeth Irving* took "a whole bunch of big shots" on its first run up the Fraser River from New Westminster, "we had to be out there with a band."[130] So it went for a formative decade in the life of Irene's father.

ON HIS OWN

Leaving, at age sixteen, the only home he had known for a decade, Cornelius Kelleher perforce made his own way without familial support apart from that of the priests. To do so, he drew on what he had learned in school, which meant fairly menial jobs demanding brute force far more than they did sophisticated work skills. "My first job... I felled trees and helped... make skids on which we hauled out the logs with a bull team."[131] Cornie learned to survive in the world of work.

All well and good, but the short and long term were very different from the perspective of the priests who had brought Cornelius up. The various stories about how he acquired land imply that they wanted to give him a material base for settling down and thereby being able to take a wife. Cornie explained in a 1957 interview: "In 1893 I bought a farm from the Bishop. In former days a priest had pre-empted the property and turned it over to the church. In that way the Bishop acquired a great deal of Matsqui Prairie area."[132] The land, located in an area known as Ridgedale just across the Fraser River from the priests' school, was owned by the Catholic bishop at the time it was acquired by Cornie.

Irene had a less sanguine explanation. She understood that when her father left St. Mary's Mission he was given land and had a house built for him.[133] The reason was that "my dad was granted the deed to this property in place of the property owned by his father, Mortimer Kelleher, on the bank of the Fraser River," which had been taken over by the priests on Mortimer's death.[134] "The OMI gave him 80 acres of land on the south side of the Fraser River.... This deed of land was 'change' so to speak from his father's sold estate, less his room and board."[135] Cornelius built a frame house on the property with two rooms upstairs at a cost of $250 for lumber and a carpenter.[136]

Having either purchased or been bequeathed property, Cornelius set out to farm, using ducks and deer as a food supply. His plans were upset by his second big flood experience. The first had occurred in 1882. The larger boys at the mission school had to round up the semi-wild cattle after the dyke broke and to ferry them across the river.[137] In the big Fraser River flood of 1894, Cornelius paddled his canoe through his window to the stairs, which he then used to get to his bedroom where he cooked and slept.[138] The high water created a shortage of feed and, to meet the hard times, Cornelius secured work repairing the railway. Afterwards, he headed up to the Nechako, near present-day Kitimat, with a friend to search for gold, only to discover that they were too early in the season, and so they returned home. They then fished for salmon for a cannery at New Westminster and helped build a cold storage plant there.[139]

Dispatched to St. Mary's Mission school on his mother's departure, followed by his father's death, Cornelius Kelleher grew to manhood in an institutional setting moderated by a sense of community with fellow students and, to some extent, by his being favoured by those in charge. Mission Community Archives MCA—0228 0018027

Cornelius was determined to better himself, and in doing so, he acquired a thirst for adventure. In 1895, he went north to the Queen Charlotte Islands, now Haida Gwaii, to catch halibut before heading to the Fraser River to fish for salmon. That winter he and a partner returned to the farm, where they hunted game, both for meat and to sell to the steamers plying the Fraser River. In the summer of 1896, they fished for salmon, but a year later, Cornelius, perhaps with stories from his father in his head, was determined once more to prospect for gold and headed off with two partners to Chilliwack Lake. But again the expedition did not pan out.[140] Cornelius gave every appearance of becoming one of the numerous male rovers who never quite settled down into family life. Indeed, he would reflect in old age that one of the consequences of getting married was that thereafter he "must stay closer to home."[141]

IRENE'S MATERNAL INHERITANCE

The woman Cornelius Kelleher would wed, Julia Mathilda Wells, was in her early years equally as adventurous as her husband. Mattie, as she was known, shared both publicly and with her daughter, Irene, many dimensions of an upbringing similarly fractured. Like Cornie, Mattie was alone from a young age, but in very different circumstances.

Julia Mathilda Wells was born on October 14, 1876, at Hatzic in the Fraser Valley, not far from where her future husband then lived.[142] "My father was Joshua Willard Wells from Jackson County, Michigan, of Welsh descent."[143] Her paternal grandfather, she was told, had trained in Wales as a civil engineer prior to emigrating to the United States.[144]

SETTLING AT PORT DOUGLAS

Born in 1828, the young Joshua Wells was, like so many others, captivated by the California gold rush and subsequently migrated north in pursuit of newer finds.[145] As explained by his daughter Mattie, he landed in British Columbia, but "like a lot of the rest of them, didn't make anything." As Mortimer Kelleher had done, Joshua Wells decided the time had come to turn his hand to something else. He decided to do so at Port Douglas, a major transit point at the north end of Harrison Lake on what was for a time a principal route to the goldfields. There, according to his granddaughter Irene, he ran "a kind of a hotel or stopping place."[146] By her father's account, it was a saloon, perhaps a boarding house, possibly something of all three.[147]

At Port Douglas, Joshua Wells partnered with a local Indigenous woman named Ki-ka-twa or Julia. Irene described her as "a full blooded native Indian, having come from the tribe at Port Douglas" and one of Peter Douglas's two children.[148] According to Julia's daughter Mattie, as she heard the story: "When a girl of about 15 she and several other girls were stolen for slaves by the Yale tribe. But they were able to escape and walked home over the mountains. My father and mother were married in Pt. Douglas and 3 children were born there."[149] Irene may have been more honest in describing her maternal grandparents as "only married in Indian fashion."[150] The three oldest children, Sarah Jane, John Joshua, and Chester Philip, were born in 1863, 1865, and 1870, so far away from the newcomer world that their births were not legally registered.[151]

MOVING TO ST. MARY'S MISSION

By the beginning of the 1870s, the once boom town of Port Douglas had collapsed because the route to the goldfields on which it sat was no longer being used, and so Joshua Wells moved on. His future son-in-law, Cornelius Kelleher, explained how "he took his house down and loaded two large canoes."[152] According to Mattie, "mother just carried the baby and he [Chester, the youngest child] was only three weeks old when they came down the river" from Port Douglas along Harrison Lake and then down the Harrison and Fraser Rivers.[153] Speculating on the choice of destination, their granddaughter Irene noted how "Grandfather Wells would have been one of the early miners that went up to the Cariboo, so he would have known about the land along the [Fraser] river."[154]

Joshua Wells and his family set down around St. Mary's Mission at the beginning of 1872, near to Mortimer Kelleher, who had come in 1864, and also close to recent arrival Michel Lacroix.[155] On December 23, 1869, Lacroix had pre-empted 160 acres "situated about 1 mile above St. Mary's Mission on the north bank of the Fraser River" that he would in 1886 turn into a Crown grant.[156]

Michel Lacroix had left Montreal in 1839, aged eighteen, to work for the Hudson's Bay Company in New Caledonia, today's central British Columbia. For a time, he was stationed at remote Fort Babine about a hundred kilometres north of present-day Smithers, where he partnered with a local Babine woman named Catherine Pookrvietak. A namesake son was born in 1854, Gabriel two years later. They were followed by four more children.[157] In 1869, Lacroix, according to Mattie, "brought his family down here to get educated."[158] Sadly, he died four years later, leaving Catherine and their six children to fend for themselves.[159] The Lacroix family survived, but did not fulfill their father's hopes for them. "They never went to school, just the girls went to school down at the convent in Mission." As for the boys, they "managed to write their names, and that was all."[160]

On January 8, 1872, Joshua Willard Wells pre-empted 160 acres "near St. Mary's Mission commencing from a stake on the north bank of the Fraser River adjoining Lacroix's claim on its east side."[161] The property, which Wells would turn into a Crown grant in 1884, ran "right down to the [Fraser] river and right down to Hatzic Lake."[162] Initially the location was known as Wells' Landing, but, according to Joshua's son-in-law Cornelius Kelleher, "they changed it from Wells' Landing to Hatzic when the Canadian Pacific Railway come through."[163]

Like the others, the Wells family sought self-sufficiency. Mattie explained how, on their farm, "they had a lot of sheep and a lot of pigs, and of course cattle." She remembered that her father "planted every little bit of clearing he had, he planted fruit. There's an awful lot of apple trees. Apple trees, and plum trees, and cherry trees, and peach trees, and walnut trees.... Every little place that he'd clear, he'd put an orchard.... Oh, he had big orchard. The orchard down on the flat, an orchard upon the next bench." It was not only fruit trees. "My, he had a nice patch of grapes. Built a great big place with a lot of nice grapes. But we didn't do nothing with those grapes. We'd just eat them, of course, and our friends come around." There was more to the story.

> He used to take things to the fair all the time. He used to
> raise watermelons, moss melons, and all those cucum-
> bers, pumpkins, great big pumpkins. He used to take that
> to the Chilliwack fair. He found those great for sheep. He
> seen a nice ram that he wanted. So he traded the pumpkin
> for this ram. Just even trade. And the other fellow got the
> prize, of course.[164]

All the hard work, and perhaps a bit of dreaming, did not have its just rewards. The all-important trees would not prove profitable. Wells and his neighbours tried to sell their produce, but "they couldn't even make freight out of it." Markets were too far away. There was a simple, if unprofitable, solution: "So they just quit and people just helped themselves. There were a lot of neighbours around and [they would] come and get grafts and fruit… but they couldn't really make a living out of it." So Wells looked to other means of making a livelihood. "The main thing was his sheep and pigs."[165] Wells was inventive, his granddaughter recalling how "he was always trying out new things."[166] According to Irene, who, when I knew her, still had some proudly in her possession, her grandmother Julia Wells "made trade baskets."[167]

A community grew up around St. Mary's Mission. Kelleher had set his family down to the west of it, Wells and Lacroix to the east.[168] Unlike the soon-to-be-fatherless Lacroix family, the Wells family grew in size. James Darius was born in 1872, Amos Louis in 1873, and then Julia Mathilda in 1876.[169] Mattie described how Joe Deroche's "wife was my godmother," just as she had been of her future husband.[170] Irene's parents were so linked virtually from their births.

FAMILY DISRUPTION

Julia Wells was pregnant again when the family was disrupted. The impetus may have been fairly prosaic—the sort that occurs within most couples from time to time. Mattie once explained to Irene what had happened: "Her mother and father had separated when she was just a baby—not even weaned. But her mother wouldn't nurse her and because her mother and father quarreled her mother left home and so her sister was left with the care of her little baby sister."[171]

As Irene understood the sequence of events, the cause lay in differing understandings of their bodies by females and males. "Grandmother left her husband when he got mad that she would not feed the baby," but "she wouldn't because she was already pregnant with Uncle Andrew," who would be Irene's violin-playing uncle.[172] Julia did not have enough milk for baby Mattie and was bawled out for what she could not do, so she walked out.[173] Irene would later take pride in that, unlike a lot of Indigenous women living with newcomer men, "she wasn't pushed out, she got out on her own."[174] After fifteen years and six children together, with a seventh on the way, the relationship had run its course.

As is often the case, a surface misunderstanding obscures deeper differences driving a couple apart. As Irene explained to me, her maternal grandparents had only been married "Indian custom."[175] The unwillingness of the various churches to receive such persons into their fold may have played a role in the separation, for as Irene shared: "I think maybe that was the trouble with them having separated when they did, because Grandmother Wells then joined the Roman Catholic Church. Grandfather Wells was with the Methodists, and I don't think he (the preacher) was agreeable to this [Indian] marriage."[176]

Whatever the mix of reasons, the union was over. "So anyway, they quarreled, so she left Grandpa Wells, and she went to live down by the bank [of the Fraser River], and the Indians would come and they would always visit and so she did go with the other Indian families that were down there."[177] Julia's seventh and final Wells child, Andrew, was born in March 1878.[178] According to Irene, "she kept him so he learned the language" perhaps because, according to one story, "Grandfather Wells would not claim him" as his child.[179] Eventually Julia formed another relationship and had two more daughters.[180]

Julia's departure from the Wells family, likely in late summer 1877, left six children without a mother. Sarah Jane, the eldest at age fifteen, already was or then became a student at St. Mary's Mission.[181] Next came four boys aged between four and twelve for whom their father took responsibility.

That left Julia Mathilda, not yet a year old when her mother left, and here it was, as often happened during these years, the wider community came to the rescue. Irene explained to me how "Mrs. Wade took mother."[182] The Wellses and the Wades were almost certainly already acquainted. A Cariboo miner from Quebec, Frank Wade had in 1871, while in his mid-thirties, married an Indigenous woman a few years his junior, Kate Chastagua. Like Mattie's mother, Kate was from Port Douglas.[183]

The Port Douglas route to the goldfields having been abandoned, Wade opened a store at the point where steamers on the Fraser River landed to accommodate both settlers and Indigenous people.[184] Irene described ensuing events, as the story had been related to her by her mother:

> Mrs. Wade came to visit and found this little girl without its mother, so she took the little one to her home and mother said she slept in the top tray of a trunk. Mother remembered much of Mr. & Mrs. Wade who lived up the river from Hatzic about 15 miles [24 kilometres] or so on the south side of the river on the bank of the Fraser River, known as Wade's Landing. Here Mr. Frank Wade kept a store, and here homesteaders from Sumas Prairie walked over a trail on Sumas Mountain to buy their supplies, as well as those who lived on the river from Nicomen, and south or down the river. Mother must have lived with them for a few years for she remembers carrying water from the river to water the garden—she was paid ten cents a pail. She remembers that Mrs. Wade was very strict and taught my mother to respect and speak properly to their elders, saying, "Yes, mam, no mam." She also corrected her

husband, who in the first place would have had to teach her the English language. But of course respect for elders would have been naturally inborn in her as an Indian.[185]

At some point in time, Mattie Wells was returned home or more likely went to live with her older sister Sarah Jane. "I stayed with my sister most of the time, you see. She got married, and then I stayed with her a lot."[186] In 1879, when Mattie was three, Sarah Jane married the proverbial boy next door, Gabriel Lacroix. He was twenty-three compared with her sixteen years, a common age disparity in first marriages then. As to their mothers' identities, his was described on their marriage certificate as "Catherine Indian woman," hers as "Julia Indian woman."[187] The couple took up a homestead near their families.

Asked later in life what she remembered most about her early childhood, Mattie responded—likely as her siblings would have done—"Just seemed to be always work. Always had to work, watch the cows, and run for the cows. Get up early in the morning and go and chase the cows in. Help milk and make butter once in a while. Help around the house."[188] Whether it was living with the Wades, with her father and brothers, or with her much older sister, Mattie did not much speak of family life, likely because there was so little of it.

IN THE MATTER OF SCHOOLING

For the young Mattie Wells, there was also the matter of schooling, or rather the lack of it. Like their Lacroix neighbours, her older brothers had very little, if any, formal education—not surprising, given the difficult circumstances in which they grew up. Irene remembered about her oldest uncle, "Josh never attended a regular school—his father taught him to read."[189]

Mattie Wells' early schooling was "very irregular," to quote her daughter.[190] To the extent that she attended school at all, it was when she and likely one or more of her brothers lived with Sarah Jane subsequent to her marriage, but even then it was not easy to do. Remembering the route from her older sister's home to her first school, Mattie noted: "We walked on the ground and then we'd go up a tall ladder, and then get on that CPR bridge, and then go to Dewdney school."[191] The Dewdney public school was memorable not only for the difficulties in getting there but also because its teacher was, Irene explained, "a Miss Todd, a relative of Premier S.F. Tolmie."[192]

Describing her mother's and maternal uncles' schooling to me, Irene reflected on how an individual teacher could make a difference in countering attitudes towards persons of mixed descent. Mattie's older brother, Irene's Uncle Jim, considered he got especially good treatment because "Miss Todd was Native."[193] Irene queried me a few months later, "So who was she?"[194]

Although I did not realize it at the time Irene posed the question, she was absolutely correct in her hunch. The British Columbia public school records tell us that the Burton Prairie School opened in Dewdney in 1882. Its teacher from 1883 to 1886 was Catherine Tod, who was indeed of mixed descent.[195] Born in 1868, her grandfathers were Scottish Hudson's Bay Company officer John Tod and Scottish ordinary employee Donald Macaulay. Her grandmothers were respectively a mixed-descent fur trader's daughter and a Tsimshian woman. The relationship with BC premier Simon Fraser Tolmie about which Irene speculated was not one of blood, but rather that they shared a similar mixed descent. The premier's father was another Scottish Hudson's Bay Company officer, his mother the daughter of an officer and a woman of mixed French-Canadian and Flathead descent.

EVERYDAY LIFE FOR GIRLS AT ST. MARY'S MISSION SCHOOL

Mattie Wells' pathway from public school to St. Mary's Mission followed that of her older sister, Sarah Jane, and also of the neighbouring Lacroix daughters, all of whom were students there for a time. Mattie attended St. Mary's Mission school as a day pupil and intermittently.[196] "They put me down in the convent in the OMI, you see, where the sisters were. I was there for a little while. The nuns there were very good. They learned the girls lotta things. To sew and cook and do fancy work."[197]

In attending the mission school, Mattie acted in opposition to her father's wishes: "Mother was a Catholic and our father was a Methodist, those days and, of course, he didn't want me to go to Catholic school. He wanted me to go to Protestant school."[198] Not only that, Irene recalled, she "attended her church at St. Mary's Roman Catholic Church," perhaps at her absent mother's instigation.[199] Mattie returned briefly to public school, "then back to the convent," she explained. "That's the way I changed 'round.... Just a little while at every school. I guess that's why we didn't get to learn much of anything."[200]

Young Cornelius Kelleher's romance with fellow St. Mary's Mission student Mary Ann Purcell was thwarted by her Irish-born father, depicted on the centre right in front of the trading post he ran in Port Douglas on an abandoned route to goldfields. Determined his daughter would not wed a "half-breed" like Cornelius—though she was of mixed descent herself—he offered a $10,000 dowry to the first white man making it to Port Douglas for that purpose, and the race was on. Royal BC Museum and Archives, A-00792

Like her future husband, Madeleine Wells was, by virtue of her intermittent life at St. Mary's Mission school, caught up in a generational cohort. Some of Mattie's fellow students, or their predecessors or successors, are visible in the 1881 census, complemented by a list of fellow students compiled by a boarder who was there from 1874 to 1884.[201] Upwards of thirty-five girls were enrolled at any one time, either off and on like Mattie or for their entire childhoods.[202] While Mattie knew some of them second-hand, others would become lifelong friends or were already friends, as were the two youngest Lacroix daughters, Ellen and Mary, who were nine and three years Mattie's senior.[203]

Mattie was likely acquainted with Catherine and Mary Ann Purcell, whose well-educated father had stayed on in Port Douglas after others, like Mattie's family and the Wades (who had rescued her as an infant) left for the Fraser Valley. Born in Cork, Ireland, in 1815, George Goodwin Purcell had, like so many of the gold miners, arrived via California and, once the rush ran its course, decided the time had come to settle down. Catherine and Mary Ann were the two oldest daughters among eight children he had with a Port Douglas woman named Mary Kreayary.[204] Left "the only white settler at Douglas," Purcell operated a trading post at which the Lower Lillooet people exchanged furs for goods. He also had a farm and an orchard.[205]

A number of Mattie's fellow students, or students she knew about, had brothers on Cornelius's side of the fence, as with Mary and Florence Baker, who were just a year or two older, and Fanny Cunningham, ten years Mattie's senior. At age six, in May 1871, when her father was a saw filer at the Hastings Mill on Burrard Inlet, Fanny had been enrolled in the socially prestigious St. Ann's Academy in New Westminster. Fanny was likely there until the spring of 1875, when, according to the family, his accidental death from slipping on winter ice meant no more money for fees.[206] So, at about age thirteen, she was dispatched to the much more ordinary St. Mary's Mission.[207] There, according to a long-time Mission resident, "the nuns worked her in the kitchen and doing the sewing."[208]

Transferred on her father's death from the prestigious St. Ann's Academy in New West-minster to the much more ordinary St. Mary's Mission, Fanny Cunningham would wed fellow student Henry Edwards, son of a Welsh naval officer enticed by gold and of an Indigenous woman, to have thirteen children together. Mission Community Archives, MCA-GPC-023A-022

JOSEPHINE HUMPHREYS' PATHWAY

Among Mattie's schoolmates, none engenders more empathy than does her lifelong friend Josephine Humphreys. Josephine's story, which she wrote down in her old age, and which her granddaughter Rosemarie, whom she raised, shared with me the better to tell both Irene's and Josephine's stories, embodies very real pathos.[209]

Born in Liverpool in 1840, Josephine's father, Thomas Basil Humphreys, was another of the many thousands of gold rush arrivals. Reaching Victoria by coastal steamer from California in July 1858, he claimed to have been a cadet in the East India Company, a British company trading in Asia, which, whether overstated or not, got him appointed as a constable.[210] Humphreys served briefly at Hope in the Fraser Valley, where he partnered with a Chehalis chief's daughter named Lucy Semo, then at Port Douglas during its gold rush heyday.[211]

In May 1862 a visiting Anglican bishop reported in his personal journal under the stark heading "Immorality [underlining in original]" how "almost every man in Douglas lives with an Indian woman," including Humphreys. According to the bishop, "the Indian woman he lived with was named Lucy, by whom he had a child." The bishop described how the local magistrate sent Humphreys away on business, promising to take care of Lucy and baby Tommy while he was gone, but instead the magistrate "violated the promise & induced the woman to come to him."[212]

The couple must have gotten back together again, for five years later Tommy acquired a sister named Josephine: "I was born at Seaton Lake [one hundred kilometres north of Port Douglas] June 16, 1868 in a mining camp tent. My father [was] Thomas Basil Humphreys, mother Lucy Semo, older daughter of the chief of the Chehalis, a well known and respected native."[213] The youngest of the couple's three children was Edward or Eddie, born in about 1870 in the gold-mining enclave of Lillooet, 160 kilometres north of Port Douglas.[214] Josephine recalled her first four years as idyllic.

An ambitious Thomas Basil Humphreys arrived in the Fraser Valley during the gold rush. He was appointed a constable at Hope, where he partnered with a Chehalis chief's daughter, Lucy Semo, ca. 1870. Royal BC Museum and Archives, A-0137

> My father mined for gold. As children we lived in a small
> house in Lillooet, father a police officer.... Voices linger of
> Father with Tommy, Eddie, and I'd say prayers and sing
> hymns. He taught me how to watch and pray to be rejoic-
> ing every happy day, happy day when Jesus washed my
> sins away. Jesus loves me, I can hear his voice. Yet many
> happy days.

That was not all. "A Chinese merchant, July we called him, was a
kind fellow. I grieve the rice cookies and candies, fire crackers etc. he
gave us, always kind. Dick Hoey or Hoy."[215]

Life was not, however, as it seemed to the small child. Humphreys
was captivated by politics, due, according to his obituaries, to his "pleas-
ing presence and impressive, winning voice." [216] In 1868, he became a
member of the British Columbia colonial legislature for Lillooet, a position that brought with it a certain cachet and likely a tendency to want
to conform to the status quo. "He aspired for power and influence," so
one of his obituaries summed him up.[217] Josephine repeatedly told the
story of how her father asked her mother to go with him to the colonial
capital of Victoria, but "she knew she would not be accepted because
she was a full-blooded Indian so she declined and stayed on non-Indian
land beside the [Chehalis] reserve, and so later he got a British wife."[218]
For Josephine, the important point was that her beloved father had not
abandoned her, but rather been compelled by circumstances to act as he
did. Whatever the actual situation, the consequences rebounded on the
young child: "Then the time came when we had to leave mother, grief,
bewilderment, all too soon.... Too young to remember. Left Mother Feb.
1872."[219]

The three Humphreys children were separated. As Josephine
explained, "the two boys, Tommy and Eddie, were sent to board with
an 'up country' family. That was my last memory of them."[220] The 1881
census tells us that Tommy was dispatched to a Scots farmer in the
Lillooet area with an Ontario-born wife and two very young children.

Eddie went to a nearby farming family headed by an Englishman and an Indigenous British Columbian woman without children of their own. Given that the brothers' father represented that area in the provincial legislature from 1871 to 1875 and had to have had contacts there, the location is not unexpected. Tommy could not be located in the 1891 census; by which time Eddie was farming in a largely Indigenous area and was the father of two very young daughters with a British Columbia–born, possibly Indigenous, woman. Thereafter both brothers slip from view in the census.[221]

As for Josephine, "my father had me in Victoria." The four-year-old spent the next two years with her father and soon also with a white stepmother.

> I then was sent to Victoria. Father remarried Carolyn Watkins. That was a grief laden memory. Still, I loved my Father who was always kind, at a time of illness had Father by my bed when I regained consciousness after a time. He was always by me, praying, I would listen, too ill to talk but after days I was better and in my mind the prayer he had repeated I could say it with him, "gentle Jesus, meek and mild, look on me a little child, pity me and pity mine, suffer me to come to thee."[222]

Even that compromise proved temporary. Humphreys' wedding on November 3, 1873, may have been less a deliberate choice than the inevitable consequence of poor judgment, for the couple's first child, named after his father, was born seven weeks later.[223] Whatever the particulars, Carolyn Watkins, the new Mrs. Humphreys, was a good catch, being the niece by marriage of a wealthy Victoria man living on "several acres" off prestigious Rockland Avenue, which on his death in 1883 became the Humphreys family's home.[224] Humphreys would sit in the colonial and then in the provincial legislature on and off till his death in 1890. His obituaries refer to only his second family.[225]

Humphreys' marriage presaged permanent separation from a daughter who was clearly loved. Whoever made the decision, Josephine's presence in this politically and socially charged household became untenable. "I was sent to St. Mary's boarding school, Sisters of St. Ann teachers, French and Irish women." On March 15, 1874, she was admitted as a boarder. The birth of a second child shortly before Humphreys became provincial minister of finance in February 1876 ensured Josephine would remain there. As she later rationalized the decision: "They had two little girls who were in Victoria with them.... We had to have a boarding school so I came to St. Mary's."[226]

Another interpretation of events is less benign. As Irene pointed out to me, while her own mother attended the mission school only as a day pupil, Josephine was a boarder because "her father abandoned her."[227] Whatever the ambiguities of her father's marriage, the transition from genteel Victoria to St. Mary's Mission was horrendous, so Josephine later recalled.

> We milled our own flour, which was coarse and almost black. Our tea was "swamp tea" made from the tiny leaves we gathered and dried. It too was black. Smoked and dried eulachon were one of our main sources of food. We strung the fat little fish on long sticks to smoke them, then hung them in long rows to dry. Bullrush-down filled our pillows, and sometimes served as mattresses, too.[228]

All her life Josephine identified the mission with hard work and poor health: "Much illness I had there.... Got cold when forced to be out in icy water hanging laundry out, that left me underweight for a long time."[229] As explained to me by Josephine's granddaughter Rosemarie, who spent long periods of time with her, "if she didn't know well enough [to work], they were hit over the back with the hoe." More generally, "Josephine used to tell about how badly treated she was in school by the nuns."[230]

In part responsible for Josephine's attitude towards the mission was how much she "wanted to be with her father, but at the same time understood that there was no place for her when he remarried."[231] Others saw her circumstances quite differently: "She could read and knew all the fine points of etiquette. When her father remarried an English woman she was put in St. Mary's mission school. The nuns were very good to her and never made her do hard work." From this perspective, she "was raised by the nuns to be [a] lady."[232] Josephine had mellowed in old age and reflected on how "the good sisters of St. Ann, my teachers, taught us to live truthfully, honestly, faithful."[233]

MATTIE'S MIGHTY ADVENTURE

Just as St. Mary's served different purposes for different students, pupils departed the school in various ways.[234] Whereas Mattie's future husband, Mortimer Kelleher, left St. Mary's for the world of work, she had a mighty adventure.

In the summer of 1889, not quite thirteen years old, Julia Mathilda Wells left the Fraser Valley in a fashion rare among her contemporaries, most of whom stayed fairly close to home and were possibly still in school. Mattie's mighty adventure would give her a resourcefulness and a confidence in her own capacity to survive under difficult circumstances that would serve her well throughout her life.

The impetus lay in Mattie's older sister, Sarah Jane, who had cared for Mattie after their mother departed, and in Sarah Jane's husband, Gabriel Lacroix, who was restless and ambitious. During the construction of the western terminus of the transcontinental Canadian Pacific Railway in the early 1880s, the couple opened a boarding house and store not far from Wade's Landing. They started a salmon drying and salting plant, stored ice cut from the Fraser River in an ice house that was lined with sawdust brought by steamboat from a New Westminster sawmill, and shipped fresh salmon east by rail. For a time before an 1886 fire destroyed much of the incipient Vancouver, they ran a fish and game store there.[235]

Another adventure was soon in the offing. About this time Gabriel Lacroix heard about a projected railway through the Bulkley Valley running north and south from today's Smithers, inland from Prince Rupert, and he "wanted to go back" to that "new country." He had good reasons to do so. His Babine mother had taught him the Wet'suwet'en language spoken across much of the north-central Interior as well as local knowledge, his fur trader father a range of practical survival skills. Mattie recalled: "My sister and her husband, they thought they'd go look for land. So they sold off their little store [near Wade's Landing], they sold that out and left their place.... Quite a lot of freight they had 'cuz they were going to do a lot of trading.... 'Cuz he could talk the language and understand 'em."[236]

Mattie was taken along. "I should've been to school. Ha!... But then they wanted me to be with my sister, 'cause she'd be alone."[237] Mattie's older brother Jim, aged about nineteen, also went, likely because he had been working for his brother-in-law in his store.[238] Mattie recalled the trip north: "In 1889 I went with my sister and her husband, Gabriel Lacroix, and my brother Jim to New Westminster by CPR. Then by steamer to Victoria. Thence on an excursion trip to Pt. Essington, on the 'Islander' for a $10.00 fare."[239]

In interviews Mattie did in her eighties, in 1957 and 1963, she described her youthful adventure in vivid detail.[240] Arriving at Port Essington, located on the mouth of the Skeena River south of present-day Prince Rupert, the foursome went to see the knowledgeable and well-known Irish-born local trader Robert Cunningham. "He told them where to get canoes" and so they "put their freight into that" for the next stage of the trip.[241]

Port Essington was only the beginning of the mighty adventure. "From there were 13 days travelling by canoe up the Skeena river to Old Hazelton," 300 kilometres northeast of Prince Rupert, where "[we] left much of our equipment." On the trip, "our Captain was Chief Kitsalas."[242] The reason was that "this Kitsalas George, [as] they called him, he was the man that owned the canoe, and then they filled the canoe up with whatever the folks had, and he had his son as captain, and one Indian as a sailor," which meant he "looked after the sails." In old age, Mattie relived the emotion of the adventure: "Oh, it was rough. Awful rough. Going up the river. And every once in a while they'd have to put a part of a sail down 'cause it was getting too rough.... We never used to paddle. Only to cross the river. There was always towing, with rope, you see. I know my brother Jim had to get out and help them to tow it."[243]

Mattie recounted in detail the trip up the Skeena River. "By canoe and portage, we journeyed to François Lake. We crossed the old Indian bridge, which was made of old telegraph wire and timbers, and still stands at Hacquilgate, one at a time. We had several pack horses that were forced to ford the river."[244] The telegraph wire out of which the bridge had been constructed was left over from a mad dash in the mid-1860s to test whether a telegraph line linking North America and Europe could be constructed more rapidly across the Pacific via north-western British Columbia or by laying a cable across the Atlantic. When the latter proved successful in 1867, wire and other equipment was abandoned where it lay.

> The Indians made that out of wire left over from [surveyor and telegrapher John] Mclure's telegraph trail. And we had to cross that one at a time. It was so rickety and you had to hang on to it on the sides. My sister's husband, he had to take his shoes off 'cause he was afraid to walk. Even the dogs wouldn't cross it.

The bridge became part of family folklore. "We always called it the devil's bridge."[245]

To get to their intended destination of François Lake, the quartet travelled the mighty Skeena River some 300 kilometres to the Wet'suwet'en community of Moricetown and then southwest another 200 kilometres. The Hagwilget Bridge near Hazelton was not the only seemingly insurmountable obstacle, as the group discovered on reaching Moricetown.

> And then we got to another bridge. The Indians wouldn't
> allow us across their bridge. They took the boards up. And
> they didn't want us to cross there at all, 'cause they didn't
> want us to go in there. But, anyhow, my brother Jim kind of
> quieted them down and then we got across.... It was quite
> a big bridge 'cause the horses could cross over that. That's
> the reason they wanted to stop us from going across.

Other new experiences along the way included meeting Indigenous people who "just had a blanket around them" and "totem poles, and the flags flying over all the cemeteries where they buried their dead." These were wholly new experiences for a young Mattie so far away from the familiar Fraser Valley of her childhood. "We never seen any before."[246]

What seems amazing in retrospect is that the adventurers reached their remote destination unscathed. "I don't know how many days it took us... but we got to François Lake." The location had been selected for a reason. Reflecting in the third person, Mattie explained how "they were following the Indians, you see, where they used to go hunting. And they thought perhaps there might be some good hunting grounds."[247]

Then the misunderstandings began. The Indigenous men taking the group to their destination did not intend to remain, or for the four newcomers to do so after hunting there themselves. "When they were through, they were ready to come home, [and] they didn't want us to stay there.... They wanted us to come home too."[248]

The foursome decided to take their chances and remain at François Lake. "My sister's husband felt that we should stay there and test the winter." Accommodations seemingly awaited them. "The Indians had a nice log cabin, and all stuffed up with moss, and the Indian fireplace in the middle." It was then difficulties began.

> The Indians didn't want us to stay. But anyhow, we stayed;
> my brother, my sister, and I stayed there. And her husband
> was supposed to go out and get some more provisions. So
> they all went out together, and they kept goin', kept going,

three weeks. Four weeks. They stayed there three months. And we just had to count everything right down to our little potatoes and fish. And of course, there's lot of rabbits.[249]

It turned out Mattie's brother-in-law Gabriel Lacroix, who had been the impetus for the adventure and the only one knowledgeable about the region, had taken off with the men who had brought the foursome there. Irene likely reflected her mother's feelings when she explained how "auntie's man," who Irene described as "a bad man," abandoned them, "supposedly to look for supplies." In effect, "Gabe Lacroix skipped out with all the stuff and went back to Hazelton."[250]

Left to their own resources without the expertise Gabriel Lacroix possessed by virtue of having lived in that part of British Columbia and on that basis having instigated the trip, the three Wells siblings somehow survived the winter on remote François Lake. Mattie explained how they averted disaster.

> My brother would go out hunting every day. But he had to be careful about ammunition. 'Cuz it was scarce you know. There was nowhere to get it. 'Cuz there was no place around there we could go, and we was there three months.... My brother had quite a time. Out every day, sometimes he'd find some dried fish [in an Indian cache] and he'd bring that home. And he killed a swan one time. And the breast lasted for I don't know how many meals.

As for the dried fish Jim found, "we had to soak that fish for about a week, it was so dry, but it was all right," and "we's there three months, living on this stuff." It was not just Jim that did the foraging. Wood for fires had to be got.

> My sister and I go out every day and she'd cut the trees down, and we'd haul 'em down, pullin' 'em under our arms and haul 'em down to—it was a hill in the back—so it was easier to take down and she'd cut the wood and we'd pack

it in 'cause my brother couldn't be in there. He had to be
out rustling around, he'd go miles, to look for something.

The saving grace was "a deck of cards and we could play Saul once
in a while."[251] How this game was played has not been possible to determine.

In the spring, Mattie, Sarah Jane, and Jim, by now closely bound
together in their everyday lives, were rescued by local Indigenous people who had come to hunt, as they did on an annual basis. "When they
did come along,... they thought we might be dead. Anyway we weren't
dead, we's just still alive." The three Wells siblings stayed at François
Lake until June, when the hunters were ready to leave, and then travelled
with them to Hazelton through an area that had no non-Indigenous settlers, "just the Indian villages."[252] This way they did not have to recross
the devil's bridge, but instead walked to the Bulkley River, where they
got a canoe.

Reconciliation with Mattie's errant brother-in-law did not go well.
"All we had was our clothes when we got back to Hazelton," for Gabe
Lacroix had sold off everything they had left there. Not only that, "he was
making trouble up there, so they put him in jail." The three Wells siblings
left for home without him. It took Sarah Jane, Jim, and Mattie a day and
a half to reach Port Essington, where Cunningham gave them a cabin to
stay in. "Oh he was a nice old man. Showed us all his furs and everything
he had upstairs... and he used to have us down there for meals once in
a while."[253]

Then came the trip down the coast. "We managed to get home, any-
how. We got a boat.... We had to come to Nanaimo" because "the small-
pox was raging in Victoria." Jim headed there all the same, where he got
quarantined, and Mattie's sister had to sell the "odd little furs" she'd
accumulated over their winter at François Lake to rescue him. "Anyway
we got home safe and sound. We come to Vancouver then and come up
on the train and got home. And nobody knew we was coming home."[254]

A RESILIENT YOUNG WOMAN

The elder Wells was still living at Hatzic when the resilient Mattie got back home in 1890. She did not return to St. Mary's, but for the most part lived with her father, as did some of her unmarried brothers, at least from time to time. "It was nice being there."[255] Wells did not have much luck keeping housekeepers for his motherless brood. "He got women coming up from New Westminster, but they could not stand the boys; Grandfather Wells was a good cook," so it was all right.[256] Mattie's return was a boon. "When I came back I didn't go to school at all. I just kept house."[257] She also visited around. When the Canadian census was taken in the spring of 1891, both Mattie and her younger brother, Andrew, were living with Gabriel and Sarah Jane Lacroix, who had reconciled, likely on their homestead.[258] Andrew would later live with Irene's parents.[259]

Joshua Wells, who, in a posed portrait that proudly hung on Irene's wall, appears to be a typical well-suited man of the era with the expected watch chain across his vest and a goatee, had become an important presence in the community that grew up around Wells' Landing, renamed Hatzic.[260] "There always seemed to be people staying in the house."[261] Although Wells was Methodist, while his children were Catholic due to their mother's influence, Anglican Rev. George Ditcham, who worked for a time as a missionary with the Society for the Propagation of the Gospel, stayed with Wells whenever he was in the locality. While there, he taught some of the Wells sons to fiddle, which made them very popular at dances.[262]

Mattie recalled about her community-minded father: "The preachers always come around, and they had a service in his house all the time. So a few years after he gave an acre for their church... and he gave that acre for the church, English church, and then, when they wanted a cemetery, he give an acre for their cemetery at Hatzic."[263] In 1890, the first Anglican church was built on land donated by Wells, who had clearly become an Anglican, given that he would later serve as sexton.[264] During the 1894 Fraser River flood, the Wells house became a refuge.

A neighbour's daughter recalled how she first met seventeen-year-old Mattie "when during the flood we moved with stock and household to Wells Landing, now Hatzic, and occupied rooms in the Wells house."[265] The same year, the local council accepted "the offer of one and a half acres made by Mr. Wells for the purpose of a cemetery."[266] By 1896, Wells had 141½ acres left of his original 160 acres.[267]

Born in 1876 to an American come with the gold rush and a Port Douglas woman named Ki-ka-twa or Julia, Irene's mother, Mattie Wells, was at age thirteen taken along by her older sister and brother on a mighty adventure across northern British Columbia that would encourage an independent spirit, establishing her financial independence as a seamstress prior to wedding Cornelius Kelleher in 1898. Mission Community Archives, MCA-GPC018-0024

Young Mattie Wells worked for a living, especially after she had passed the usual age for marriage in the mid-teens. "Mother and sister taught me to sew," and later Sarah gave her a treadle-operated sewing machine. Mattie was determined to become proficient at sewing as a prelude to a possibly independent life. "As I felt I needed more knowledge of sewing before starting out as a seamstress, I went to New Westminster and studied with a Mrs. McFadden," who had a dress shop. While there, "Mrs. Ditcham, the Anglican Bishop's wife," would pick her up each Sunday morning to go "to my church" and "later I would go to church with her." Then, "after returning to my home I went to various homes and sewed."[268] A daughter of the Page family, which had arrived from Nova Scotia in 1890 and settled across the Fraser River from Hatzic, and had been given temporary accommodations by the Wells family during the 1894 flood, remembered:

> I recall her coming to our home in the spring of 1895 to sew for my mother. My younger sister and I were delighted to go to Page's Landing to meet her as she came off the steamer. I can still see us hopping along beside her and chattering most joyously. And how we enjoyed her pleasant manner toward two little girls.[269]

Mattie was just over twenty when the last remnants of her childhood slipped away. Her father, Joshua Willard Wells, became ill, and it was Mattie's school friend Josephine, by now experienced in caregiving, who "took over" by bringing him to her house up the hill. In her handwritten memoir, shared with me by her granddaughter, Josephine described what ensued.

> Got Dr. Walker from New Westminster to come and examine him. He told me to be careful. He sent disinfectants, rubber gloves, a chart as to what to feed and care for Willard Wells. I did as told, was able to get him to his feet, a few steps out in front room while I did his bedding and

room fixed for him. All fine when next the Dr. was up. A pleasant patient, ready to do as I asked him. I had to keep the children away from that part of the house, quite easy as it was also built apart from our quarters, up a few steps so babies could not get up…. We all managed very well, I think.[270]

Wells died on November 25, 1898.[271] Her siblings busy with their own lives, the resourceful Mattie was now fully on her own, which she had been to some extent since her birth.

THE SECOND
GENERATION JOINED
TOGETHER

During the same years that Irene's parents were reaching adulthood, many of their schoolmates from St. Mary's set out on life courses that were possibly, possibly not, to their liking. They were subject to the decision made by those in charge that they be joined together in marriage prior to their departure into the world. As was generally the case in residential schools, the religious imperative that legitimized the institutions took priority over all else. Those in charge considered it their right and obligation to maintain over former students the same kind of moral authority they exercised within the school. The key to doing so lay in marrying students off, either to each other or to other acceptable persons, prior to, upon, or soon after their departure.

CONTROLLING ADULTHOODS

Race and religion coincided in controlling adulthoods. Because the religiously affiliated white men and women in charge of St. Mary's Mission could not accept their mixed-race and Indigenous charges as their equals, they were determined to extend their reach after students left the school. In consequence, even though it was the conversion of their charges to Catholicism that gave St. Mary's Mission its rationale, the school withheld from them until they were married an element essential to their "salvation," as was proclaimed to students day after day, year after year. The nun who chronicled St. Mary's Mission's first years explained:

> It was a rule not to give the first communion before Indians and half-breeds (*les sauvages et metisse*) who attended the college and the convent were married, for they were exposed to being perverted if they left the school without being married.[272]

From the perspective of those in charge, even a "mixture of white blood" would not allow students to take part in this ritual made readily available to white students from about age twelve or thirteen. As a second St. Ann's nun explained: "Rather than expose the Holy Eucharist to desecration by too readily admitting their semi-savage followers to the Holy Table, they had established the custom in these B.C. tribes of making their first communion only after marriage."[273] From the perspective of the priests and nuns who ran the mission, their charges were inherently lesser beings. No matter how hard they tried, and indeed the evidence shows that Cornelius Kelleher and his contemporaries tried very hard to do everything right, they were found wanting.

Marriage, as the priests and nuns conceived the ritual by the Catholic standards of the day, was to be so far as possible between students or former students. In 1879, the bishop in charge publicly expressed his wish that St. Mary's pupils wed each other and then settle in a proposed model farming village at Matsqui, just across the Fraser River, which would serve to keep them under direct Catholic oversight.[274]

Within this framework, the participants in a triple wedding held on July 31, 1879, were offered a showcase of goods. According to a nun then at the mission who kept a diary:

> The Oblate fathers gave the three couples a start in life by giving each a section of land and a house. The wedding clothes for the brides and grooms were made at the

convent. The breakfast was given by the Oblates, and the dinner and supper by the sisters, presided over by Father Carion. In the evening he brought them to their homes.[275]

This wedding, held at just about the time that Cornelius and his sister arrived at the mission, joined "three girls, who, according to the Catholic nun recording the events, prided themselves on their adoption by the sisters," and the "three college boys who had also been adopted by the fathers." To underline the distinctiveness of the event, the witnesses to each ceremony were the other two grooms.[276]

The first of the couples married off in 1879 were Alfred Robertson, aged sixteen, and Josephine Herrling, fifteen. Alfred had been born at Fort Langley, the son of "Tom Robertson and Teleroisa, Indian woman," about whom no further information could be located; Josephine was born at "Herrlingville, below Hope, BC" to Charles Herrling and "Siamiat, Indian woman."[277] A local history describes Josephine's father as a native of Hungary who had arrived in British Columbia as a gold miner.[278] Pre-empting land on a Fraser River island that still bears his name, Herrling likely dispatched his two oldest children, Josephine and Gustav, two years her junior, to the mission following his wife's death in the early or mid-1870s.[279]

The other two unions that took place in 1879 were of the two oldest Edwards children, Henry and Mary Ellen, whose naval officer father, "Bloody" Edwards, had paid the Oblates to look after his three children prior to returning home to Wales. Mary Ellen Edwards was married off at age sixteeen to the Oblates' favourite, nineteen-year-old Charles Gardner, whose American father had provided for but never laid eyes on him. Young Gardner was thereupon given charge of the Mission's 600-acre farm on the Matsqui side of the Fraser River.[280]

The wife selected for, or by, Henry Edwards was Caroline Florence, described on their wedding certificate as born in about 1863 in the then gold-mining enclave of Douglas to Charles Florence, a Frenchman who arrived with the gold rush, and "Kakamel, Ind woman." Having at some earlier point in time been handed over to the Sisters of St. Ann, Caroline had just turned sixteen. Henry was nineteen.[281]

After Caroline died in childbirth four or five years later, Henry Edwards wed another St. Mary's student, Fanny Cunningham, who had come to St. Mary's after a stint at the Sisters of St. Ann's more prestigious counterpart in Victoria. The first of what would be thirteen children was born to them in March 1883. The talented Henry Edwards, who acted as a court interpreter of Indigenous languages and spoke them to his children, so that they would in the 1901 census give "Indian" as their first language, is remembered for hand-making twenty-three much sought-after violins he gave away and for teaching children in the Fraser Valley and North Vancouver to play the violin.[282]

JOSEPHINE HUMPHREYS MARRIED OFF

Five years later, Josephine Humphreys was set onto the same pathway. Now having spent a decade at St. Mary's, the very day that she turned sixteen, in the spring of 1884, she wed or rather, as was common parlance among her circle of friends, was "married off by the Oblates" to Henry

The son of a Welsh naval officer, Henry Edwards raised his children with Fanny Cunningham to speak "Indian" as their first language and served as court interpreter of Indigenous languages. Mission Community Archives, MCA-GPC-024A-009

and Mary Ellen Edwards' younger brother, Patrick, who, like his siblings, knew "Indian" as his first language. [283] In what may be an interesting bit of obfuscation, Josephine's marriage certificate prepared by the priest gave her age as eighteen, making her two years older than she was.[284] According to Josephine's granddaughter, who heard the story from Josephine, on reaching the age of sixteen, "she said the girls were lined up and the men picked their wives out."[285] In Josephine's words in her memoir: "Somehow I was to marry a young school boy, age about 21 or so, I married June 26, my 16th birthday, had not talked to the man. The day I was married was the most terrible time of my life. However, here I am after many changes."[286]

As if the circumstances of the marriage were not traumatic enough, following the ceremony Josephine and this man—up to then a stranger to her—had to make a long walk through "pouring rain" to reach the Dewdney farm of her new sister-in-law, Mary Ellen Edwards, who had been married off to Charles Gardner.[287] The newlyweds, who the Oblates gifted with a cow in honour of their union, would live for the next year with the Gardners.[288]

Making Do in the Everyday

Like other St. Mary's students married off to each other, Pat and Josephine Edwards, cow in hand, made do.[289] The first year the young couple saved their money from Pat's labouring jobs, and with that small stake Pat pre-empted 160 acres on the Hatzic hillside north of his brother Henry's land. There the newlyweds put up "a small log house, 18' x 24', a lean to for kitchen."[290] They ate what they produced themselves, as Josephine described in her handwritten memoir: "Small cook stove, good oven, baked bread, had good flooring, quite content, got 2 hens, bought eggs, set, had 45 [chicks] first summer, log house, had cow from OMI so all the milk and butter we needed, hens got surplus, always plenty grouse, trout."[291]

The couple each contributed to the family economy. Pat took labouring jobs when they were to be had. As recalled by Josephine about the father of her children: "I can remember Dad working for $25 a month.

Having been dispatched by her politician father, Thomas Basil Humphreys, to St. Mary's Mission, Josephine Humphreys was, in a common practice respecting Indigenous children in residential schools, married off the day she turned sixteen to Patrick Edwards, until then unknown to her, to rebound by early on establishing herself as a practical nurse, midwife, and all around caregiver. Mission Community Archives, MCA-0310-004

And we had to make that do."[292]

Just as she did for Mattie's father, Joshua Wells, Josephine would all her life tend to the ill and dying, nurture children unable to be cared for by their parents, and bring newborns into the world as a midwife. Shortly after her marriage, when she was still only sixteen and her first child a month old, her new husband's older brother, Henry, was desperate, so:

> I went to their home at Hatzic Lake, but no help yet, that was my first confinement case... baby came, no time for panic, I first had to keep calm, got plenty water on fire, this at 4 am, my baby asleep as also the newborn's older sibling Francis two years old. I had all comfortably fixed before Henry and Mrs. Johnny Buxton [the midwife] arrived. She looked over things, found everything ok, so I had breakfast for all hands. In those days a nine day a bed was a must. I had my hands full with three babies and my sister in law Fanny Edwards nee Cunningham.[293]

Josephine wrote modestly in old age how "we helped one another nursing in times of trouble, no doctor or nurse, mostly alone."[294]

Josephine was sustained during these years by her birth parents, though in quite different ways. Responding to a letter she wrote to her father not long after she had, so she would confide to her granddaughter, married "someone you don't love and don't know," Thomas Basil Humphreys sought to put the best face on events.[295] Assuring his daughter that "I have not forgotten you," he combined platitudes with prevarications as to why "circumstances beyond my power of control prevented" them from seeing each other, why he could not send any photographs at the present time due to the weather, and why he could only hope to "have it in my power, before long to do something for you and your poor brothers," with whom he acknowledged he had lost touch.[296] It seems unlikely Humphreys did so, given that his son Edward described himself at the time of his marriage as a "herdsman" around Cache Creek eighty kilometres east of Lillooet, where he and his older brother had been deposited as children.[297] In respect to Josephine's marriage, platitudes replaced honest sentiment.

> I am glad to hear that you are happy and contented with your husband, of whom you speak so well. It is far better to have an honest man who is not wealthy for your husband than a dishonest one who is wealthy. Riches have been and can be again acquired by honest thrift and industry....
> I am as ever your loving father T.B. Humphreys.[298]

Josephine would keep her father's letter all her life, to be shared with me by her granddaughter.

It was Josephine's mother, Lucy Semo, who acted rather than dissembling. When the first of Josephine's nine children died at age one, "lucky for me my Mother came to see us."[299] Living northeast of Mission at Chehalis where she had grown up, Lucy Semo would be a stabilizing force in her daughter's life. Josephine described in her memoir how "my Mother" would "come down to see us" from time to time.[300] Perhaps in part for that reason or perhaps due to their father's influence, the half-dozen oldest children to survive early childhood would, like their Edwards cousins, speak "Indian" as their first language.[301]

The more Josephine learned about her Indigenous inheritance and about Indigenous people generally, the more she wished she knew. In her memoir, she expressed her regret.

> Our homestead was used in the early days before white folks come as safety for their family in our gully quite a lot of burned rock where their camps were. Arrows and a number of carved trinkets have been found. Mother's father was chieftain, quite a fellow, in those times there were wars between the coast tribes and inland folks. I do not know Mother's age other than she was born at Fort Langley when first white folks came, likely in 1830s

or there about.... Did not learn her language much to my
sorrow as her family had their cures, roots, barks, leaves,
berries, but could not say for what ills. Mother healthy, did
all their gardening, fond of flowers, a wonderful person,
died at 88, 1925 March 21st.[302]

Josephine's marriage would endure until Pat Edwards' death in
1941, Josephine dying in 1958.[303] Lucy Semo would die in 1925, Humphreys in 1890.

IRENE'S PARENTS

Unlike some of their contemporaries, Mattie Wells and Cornie Kelleher each left St. Mary's Mission single and on their own terms. Mattie's transition to adulthood opened up choices denied to Fanny Cunningham and Josephine Humphreys. Whether or not Mattie knew Fanny and Josephine during her time at the mission, both a decade her senior, she certainly knew about them and they became acquainted on her return from the north. Their circumstances may well have influenced her determination to marry a man of her own choosing rather than one selected for her. Cornie was very possibly "prospected" by those in charge of the mission as a candidate for being married off on leaving the school, hence their provision of a land base linked to his father's holdings. Whatever the particulars, Cornelius Kelleher left the care of the Oblates a single man, Mattie the oversight of the Sisters of St. Ann a single woman. Cornie and likely also Mattie were determined to decide on their own marriages and, perhaps even more so, to celebrate it in a fashion giving clear indication they were marrying who they chose on their own terms. Their honeymoon to Seattle may have had its impetus in this decision.

ROMANTIC ENCOUNTERS

After leaving the mission, Cornie and Mattie each engaged in a greater diversity of life experiences than most young people would have at that time. By doing so, they passed the usual age for marriage among their contemporaries—nineteen or twenty for men and sixteen or so for women. They were each a half dozen years older than this. The consequence was that they did have in the interim encounters with others and, indeed, may have been drawn together on the rebound. Mattie was, according to her daughter, "friendly" with a man who "had to leave Hatzic and go across the line [to the United States], because he wasn't behaving right; they said he was a gambler."[304] Mattie had lived dangerously and lost.

Cornie's experiences with the opposite sex were more traumatic, dealing him a hard lesson in the prejudices of the age. He got involved with Mary Ann Purcell, whose father was, like his, from County Cork in Ireland and a California gold miner come north, in Purcell's case setting down at Port Douglas with a local Indigenous woman.[305] Both Cornie and Mary Ann attended St. Mary's Mission school and, however much boys and girls were physically separated, they may have been aware of each other at the time.[306]

Mary Ann's father was having none of a relationship between the pair. It may have been the relative isolation of Port Douglas that made the elder Purcell so set in his ways, but he was determined that his now twenty-five-year-old daughter would not marry a "half-breed" like young Kelleher—although it need be noted that his daughter was also of mixed descent—but rather a white man like himself.[307] The Irish-born Purcell's biases were not so limited, since he proclaimed at about the same time that "if any man will call him a Canadian, he will knock him down."[308]

Indicative of the force of such widespread attitudes, it was not sufficient for Mary Ann's father to forbid his daughter's union with Cornie. George Goodwin Purcell was also determined there would be no second opportunity for her to dally. He made it known in the shadow of Cornie and Mattie's wedding that "if his daughter married an Indian she would get nothing, but if she married a white man there was $10,000 ready for her dowry," an enormous amount of money at the time. As soon as the news of this offer got around, two serious contenders emerged, one employed as a painter by the Harrison Hot Springs hotel, the other a thirty-five-year-old Nova Scotian named Ebenezer Fales Willie Holt, described by an eyewitness to these events as "a Jew who ran a second-hand store in New

Westminster." In what was quite literally a race for Mary Ann's hand, the two suitors made it up to Port Douglas on the same steamer, as did a visiting Catholic priest who that evening "put on a magic lantern display for some 200 Indians," in which "following a few mildly attractive religious slides came many terrifying colored pictures of life in hell." The "next morning [April 19, 1898] there was celebrated the wedding of Miss Purcell and the Hebrew, and the dowry was duly paid."[309] The steamer's engineer considered that "the decision was purely with the lady's future in mind, and the settled business man was favored as against the apparently unsettled artisan."[310] Mary Ann's store-bought husband would die five years later in New Westminster, their son Frederick in 1918 in the First World War.

COMING TOGETHER ON THEIR OWN TERMS

Denied Mary Ann Purcell, Cornie thereupon turned to Mattie. The marriage of Cornelius Kelleher and Julia Mathilda Wells was their own choice, even if it was facilitated, at least indirectly, by Cornie's acquisition of land on which to settle down, thanks to the priests and nuns of St. Mary's Mission. One of the most important lessons that Cornelius and Mathilda had to have taken away from their years at the mission was an appreciation of the ambiguities of their descent. However much they distinguished themselves from the Indigenous people around them, the priests and nuns who ran the schools were able to accept children like Cornie and Mattie precisely because they shared that inheritance. Within this frame of reference, the first historian of the Sisters of St. Ann expressed implicit approval at the nuns' response to the "impertinence" of their "native and semi native" students respecting whiteness.

> Eyeing her pointedly so as to draw her attention they said, "See how proud she is of being white, how often she washes her hands." The Sister said, "If I were proud I would not be here teaching you to read and write; to be clean and nice and to love God Who made you Indian and me white."[311]

Cornie and Mattie were at the same time very much their own persons. They had persevered through difficult childhoods and youths that, instead of wounding their spirits, led to an independence of mind. They knew who they were and, while outsiders might have considered them inferior based on their mixed descent, they appear not to have done so themselves. While we cannot know what passed between the two when they came together, and it was a topic they did not discuss publicly, the consequence was a lifelong union.

SETTLING DOWN INTO MARRIED LIFE

Adventurous youths and splashy honeymoon over, Cornelius and Julia Mathilda Kelleher settled down into married life. Their social and economic priorities built on, and might be seen to have replicated, lessons learned in and out of the classroom at St. Mary's Mission and in its wake. Their friends were in good part drawn from among their schoolmates, with whom they shared a formative experience between Indigenous and white that did not have to be defended, or revealed, in order to be understood. While others may have denigrated them as half-breeds, they refused to be so diminished.

Even though the newlyweds already had a place of their own, thanks to the land Cornelius's father had long before taken up, happiness in the form of family life was slow in coming. "Our first baby, born in late 1898 did not stay long with us."[312] A Page daughter recalled how "my mother rode down to the Kellehers' on her pony with side-saddle when she heard Mattie's baby was ill; he did not survive."[313] Mortimer Willard died at six weeks of age.[314]

A second son, Albert Cornelius, arrived on June 11, 1900, at a time the danger of high water made the Kellehers' house impractical as a home. There was so much water that spring that mother and infant had to move out until it receded.[315] Under the auspices of the Matsqui Land Company, the Oblates, and farmers who had loans provided by the provincial government, it was decided to build a new dyke. Cornelius's ongoing tie to the mission is indicated by his becoming the Oblates' representative on the dyking committee.[316] "I was asked by letter by the Rt. Rev. Paul Durieu to look after the interests of the OMI."[317] The close relationship also continued in other ways. "In 1902 Bishop Dontinwell had some cattle which he brought to me and we formed a partnership with these cattle for several years."[318]

The Kellehers' house ended up on the wrong side of the new dyke. "In 1901, as our house was outside the dyke, which had been built through there in 1898, we built another house just over the dyke."[319] Cornie constructed the framed two-storey dwelling not far from a cattle barn and dairy that he also built.[320]

The house was completed in time for Irene's birth, but just so. "They moved in, like on Sunday, and I was born the next morning in the new house," arriving at 4:00 am on December 16, 1901.[321] "It must have been a mild winter because my dad rowed across the Fraser River to Mission in the middle of the night to bring a friend back to help momma."[322] Two women "attended the delivery"—"Mrs. Pat Edwards and Mrs. John O'Neil."[323] The first to arrive was Josephine Humphreys, who had earlier nursed Mattie's father and was known to her friends as Josie.[324] "My dad said mama was having such a bad time, Josie said she didn't want to be alone, so my dad had to row across the river, go up the hill, and get Mrs. O'Neill." "And he said there'd be no more children after that."[325] And there were no more.

SELF-DETERMINING THEIR WAY OF BEING

"We lived off the land." Cornie recalled how "I could fill my pockets full of shells and go out on a Saturday afternoon and get enough grouse to last us a week."[326] The Kellehers worked hard and did well, from time to time having "hired help" stay with them. They planted an orchard of apples, pears, peaches, cherries, raspberries, and blackberries.[327] "Mission was our town, and my dad always had a boat. We would walk down the dyke and walk across the bridge,... but mostly it was by boat." Initially "it was usually a row boat," but later Cornie acquired a tugboat and also a motor boat.[328]

The pleasure Cornie Kelleher took in boats extended from their utility as a means of transportation to their enjoyment, as with this vessel to which he added a cabin. Mission Community Archives, MCA-GPC018-036A

Even though Cornelius long remained friends with individual priests and brothers—"This Brother Ryan, he was a great friend of mine"—he slowly loosened his bonds with the Oblates at St. Mary's Mission.[329] His daughter, Irene, was for her part not best pleased by how "the priest would go around collecting money so that her family wouldn't have enough left for a loaf of bread."[330]

The Kellehers would eventually break with the Catholic Church. Along with Irene, they joined the theosophically oriented Rosicrucians, whose teachings they considered more attuned to Indigenous peoples.[331] Irene became an avid promoter of the powerful technocracy movement of the interwar years and was still in 1998 musing to me, "If we only had technocracy..."[332] Links to the mission lingered all the same. In old age, Mattie pointed out to a visitor: "Up here we have an apple tree we call 'the Bishop's apple' because we took a slip from one of the trees at St. Mary's Mission and grafted it. These trees were brought to the Mission from France and grafted onto wild crabapple trees."[333]

A consequence was that, rather than attending a Catholic school as their parents had, Albert and Irene went to the public Ridgedale School, which "the fathers of the families built themselves." Irene explained how "they had a bee and they built this place that was a hall and also the school." To get there, "my brother and I walked four miles to school—snow, rain, sun and whatever—no buses, wagon, or horseback rides."[334] She took pride in their attitude to schooling. "I think we hardly missed a day. Sometimes we walked, sometimes we rafted and sometimes we crawled along the fence top when the snow was deep, but we went."[335]

All the hard work on the part of Cornie Kelleher to secure the best possible schooling for his children could not spare them from a pervasive culture of discrimination based on descent that in Irene's perspective still existed at the times of our conversations during the 1990s. Irene shared how "the first day of school a girl said to me, 'You're an Indian.' I didn't know what she meant." Soon a young Irene found out what she meant: "My brother and I, we were half-breeds, we were the only half-breeds in the school."[336]

Everyday life changed when the Kelleher children were in their early teens. "My Dad had pre-empted a quarter section on the north side of Sumas Mountain overlooking Hatzic and Dewdney."[337] He had come across the site on hunting trips, and it appealed to his and Mattie's love of quiet places.[338] The site was, in Irene's words, "sequestered."[339] Whether or not the decision was also related to their desire to live as far as possible on their own terms rather than as perceived by others as set in place between Indigenous and white, it is impossible to know.

Rather than selling their existing property, "we rented the farm and moved up there in 1914."[340] Cornie, Mattie's year-and-a-half younger brother, Andrew Wells, and a neighbour carved a new house out of the woods. "My Dad cut the shakes and he had a little mill and he and Uncle Andrew cut the lumber for the flooring but every bit of that my Dad got from the woods there."[341] Only the windows and doors were store bought.[342] Irene was intimate with the house's details, and explained with pride in her autobiographical writing how "the lumber used was No. 1 grade, with consequently no knots."[343]

On an eventful day in 1914, the Kellehers' belongings were loaded on a scow and towed by Cornie's "big tug boat."[344] Mattie and Irene walked up the dyke and then along a trail made especially to get to the new house. "I remember that dad and Albert loaded our cow, team of horses and household goods on the scow and towed it up river with our boat, the *Edna F.*"[345] Some years earlier, the Kellehers' neighbours, the Pages, had brought with them from Nova Scotia a team of horses, remembered as a white stallion and a dark mare, that Cornelius subsequently purchased.[346] In January 1910, he had, in response to a statement of interest, considered selling the stallion to Kamloops rancher C.T. Cooney "for $1500 on time and $1200 cash," but no deal ensued.[347]

The two young Kellehers had to walk down and up the mountain each day in order to go to school.[348] "Albert and I still went to Ridgedale

The Kellehers' homestead on Sumas Mountain on land acquired in 1914, shown here in about 1940 with Mattie in front, reflected their "love of quiet places," to quote their daughter Irene, and very possibly a desire to make their life together so far as possible on their own terms, which began with the house's construction of wood acquired on the property. Mission Community Archives, MCA-GPC018-036A

School from there. We walked down a little trail to the railway track until the government built a road six months later."[349]

In essence, the Kellehers created for themselves a world of their own where they could live on their own terms out of view, as far as they opted to do so, of the emerging dominant society. They self-determined their way of life, one in which Irene took pride. On an early afternoon on one of our days together, Irene decided she wanted me to see "the homestead," as she called it, and, as we drove up the mountain, she explained what each aspect of it signified. They had several ways to support themselves: "They had their field and crops to get along."[350] "They were almost self-sufficient up there with their own milk, eggs, fruit, vegetables and themselves for comfort."[351] Not only that, but the "Kellehers always had a rowboat or gasoline boat to get to Mission City to shop, or to Hatzic to visit."[352]

Cornie provided for his family in various ways. He cut shingle bolts, made cedar poles from trees on his land, and from time to time got employment with public works.[353] During the Depression years of the 1930s, he erected a pump and sluice box on the mouth of the Vedder River, where both he and Mattie washed gold worth about three dollars a day. Later, Cornie helped to blow up fir stumps prior to building the Abbotsford airport.[354] As summed up by his daughter, "he was always working somewhere."[355]

VALUING WOMEN'S WORK

Mattie worked equally as hard as Cornie to sustain the family. A neighbour "always had her cook for his threshing crew."[356] A friend recalled how "she used to walk to the Ridgedale store with two ten pound lard pails full of eggs—to trade for groceries." She did so "once or twice a week" on what was "a walk of two or three miles."[357] Irene explained: "She and Auntie [Sarah Jane Wells Lacroix] often used to go fishing [on Hatzic Lake]. Mother said that is how she made her little bit of 'spending money.'"[358]

And there was the sewing, always the sewing, a skill Mattie had acquired as a young woman. "Many of my old patrons [from before I was married] brought their sewing to my home. Some of their children and other neighbours brought theirs for many years."[359] Among those doing so was one of the two Page daughters. She had met her on their landing when, as a young woman, Mattie had come to sew for their mother, and she now relied on "Mrs. Cornie." As she explained: "We rode horseback down the dyke with sewing for her to do. How we loved those visits."[360] Later, when one of the Page daughters married, she did the same thing with her own children: "To this house I frequently took my own children and they enjoyed the hospitality of this sweet woman as much as I did.... People took sewing to Mrs. Kelleher for many years."[361]

As summed up by Irene about her mother: "All through her married life she sewed for so many ladies and their children and her own family. Even after she was 80 years old she sewed."[362] From the perspective of Irene and of many others, "she was an excellent seamstress, and almost everyone in the area, and many more throughout the valley, had clothes my mother made for them."[363] Irene took special pride in how "Mother had a wonderful knack for making over dresses and coats—remodeling—making children's clothes out of men's used suits."[364] A newspaper commented at the time of the Kellehers' fiftieth wedding anniversary: "A noted needle woman, friends and neighbors have kept her busy with their needs and she has always had as much work as she could manage."[365] Irene's wardrobe in the 1990s consisted almost wholly, she proudly showed me during one of my visits, of very well-made clothes her mother had sewn for her prior to her death a quarter century earlier.

Irene recognized that much of the everyday work in which her parents engaged was monotonous and tedious. "Mother was always very, very patient, almost super humanly patient; and it stood her in good stead to do the many menial tasks she had to do on the homestead to make a home for her family."[366] Mattie gave the impression of being thankful for an everyday life so different from her tumultuous youth. "She was a most grateful person, always looking on the cheerful side of difficult situations and doing her tasks with graceful composure."[367]

On the occasion of their fiftieth wedding anniversary in 1948, Cornelius and Julia "Mattie" Kelleher were formally photographed together. Mission Community Archives, 0025-MCA334-059

There were welcome respites. "Mother enjoyed reading the history of her own BC land."[368] A friend recalled how "she seemed so well read and interested in things."[369] A lifetime teacher, Irene took pride in how her mother not only read widely but kept what Irene described as a red dictionary on a nearby table to look up any unfamiliar words.[370] "Mother was keenly interested in all things round her. Every day she looked across the river to see if there were any changes."[371]

For his part, Cornie harboured a lifelong dream of someday striking it rich. He always bought tickets on the Irish sweepstakes, likely even more often after one of the Edwards family won some money.[372] His love of the outdoors encouraged him to prospect for three or four weeks each summer.[373] Hoping to find gold in the nearby mountains, he went in that direction a number of times. Thinking back across time, the Kellehers' daughter considered theirs to have been a good life. "Years ago we just made our garden and we were content."[374]

ENGAGING WITH THE COMMUNITY

Cornie and Mattie Kelleher's years together spanned two-thirds of a century. The necessity of making a living for themselves and their children consumed much of their time and energy, but not all of it. They were also enmeshed within a larger set of interests and obligations. Irene recalled how "both my parents were active in community work," her father helping to construct the nearby Ridgedale hall and the school that she and her brother attended.[375] The program of the Ridgedale Community Club for May 1933 read:

> Hostess Mrs. C. Kelleher
>
> Role Call Pioneer Experiences [as the expected response]
>
> Speaker Mr. C. Kelleher[376]

On her death a third of a century later, in 1967, "Julia Mathilda Kelleher" was entered into the Ridgedale "Book of Memories."[377]

Asked by me how her father in particular identified himself, Irene responded without hesitation, "As a member of the community," but as to whether he was accepted as such, she said, only "to a degree."[378] Cornie and Mattie reached out despite knowing that at any point they might be rebuffed, not for what they did or did not do, but for their descent.

One of the ways in which the Kellehers served the community was by quietly taking in persons without a home. "There was always someone in the house" during the children's childhoods, including a man Irene recalled only as "Texas" and an Englishman who "was always reading books" and stayed with them until he died.[379] A woman recalled how "she would spend days" with Mattie when "she needed to relax her nerves and needed quiet therapy."[380]

Then there was young Chrissie Allard who, Irene recalled, lived for years "in the front bedroom" while working as a housekeeper for nearby families. She eventually went north to live with her older brother, Matt, near Terrace, where she "married a man who worked on the telegraph line."[381] While it is impossible to know in all these cases precisely what the situation was, with Chrissie Allard it was one mixed-descent family caring for another. Chrissie's and Matt's grandfathers were French Canadians of modest means who arrived with the fur trade, their grandmothers Indigenous women remembered only as Henriette, almost certainly Carrier, and Cecile, who was Stikine.[382] The siblings' parents had settled in Vancouver Island's Cowichan Valley, where Matt was born in 1870 and Chrissie in about 1879.[383]

The ambivalent way in which a flirtatious, white seventeen-year-old, who in the early 1890s visited her socially conscious English grandparents living nearby, described Matt Allard, then working for them, leaves no doubt but that mixed descent informed attitudes. Individuals' pride in their origins did not necessarily translate into respect by others.

> Matthew was very proud of his family! "One of the best Hudson Bay families" he would tell you. "My mother was a French half-breed & my father was too; my great-grandfather old Allard came out from Quebeck 60 years ago & my great-grandmother was an Indian Princess, she was." After which speech he would take up his hoe with a gesture of pride and plant it, deep, into the potato row.[384]

Irene was absolutely right in her recollection of the Allard siblings. Matt worked as a chainman during the survey of the Kalum Valley north of present-day Terrace and then staked out a pre-emption on the Kalum River. He also trapped in the winter and prospected in the summer. After Chrissy went north, she married a lineman who worked for Dominion Telegraph.[385]

The Kellehers' community service could be two-edged. A young Cornelius served on the Matsqui Council, beating out another local settler to represent ward 4.[386] "I was councilor in Matsqui Municipality in 1899 and 1900."[387] He recalled how he "rode horseback across Matsqui [Indian] reserve and through a trail to municipal meetings, then held in a little schoolhouse."[388] Councillors, who received sixty dollars a year, laid out the basis of a road system during Cornie's tenure. Settlers were supposed to contribute a share of the work in exchange for getting a credit for their taxes, but some claimed roadwork that they did not do or did badly, making the position of councillor a difficult one.[389]

Cornelius may not have served longer because he was perceived to be an outsider, possibly because of his Indigenous descent. The daughter of a neighbour recalled how others asked: "Who is this man Kelleher? I never heard of him."[390] In one version of the story, the wife of the loser in the election, the same woman who had just a year earlier assisted Mattie at the birth of her eldest child, berated her husband that "you let that half-breed beat you."[391] According to another account shared with me by Irene, only a very small number of people voted during the election in which Cornelius was victorious, and some people said afterwards that "a half-breed" should not have won.[392]

All the same, throughout his life Cornelius Kelleher continued to give service and even leadership to his community. When Fraser Valley politician and British Columbia premier Richard McBride arrived for a meeting at Mission about the state of the dykes, "we all went over there and got into the hall, and he said, 'What can I do for you boys?'" Cornie recalled how "I was supposed to be the spokesman," and so got up and explained: "We've got work to do. The prairie has got to be drained. All these sloughs and low places have yet got to be drained." The premier's response, as remembered by Cornie, could not have been better:

> So Dick says: "All right, boys. I'll give you five years with-
> out paying no taxes on the property." So that was a pretty
> good deal for a while. It'd give the new fellows [who had
> recently settled in the area] a chance to drain their land
> and get it under cultivation and be able to pay taxes there,
> whatever they were assessed on their land. So that was
> pretty good, yes, sir.[393]

Cornelius identified strongly with the protection of the Fraser River shoreline through dyking, and gave extra service during the 1882, 1894, 1920, and 1948 Fraser River floods.[394] His most memorable flood was

Having fought earlier Fraser River floods by dyking almost as a matter of course, Cornie Kelleher was lauded in the aftermath of the 1848 flood for his exemplary leadership in doing so. *Wigwams to Windmills,* 110

1948 when the dyking inspector asked him, he recalled, "to take charge of the east end of the Matsqui Dyke." Even though the water "rose to about 12 inches higher than the dyke," they "kept piling the sacks" of sand and the dyke held.[395] This was no mean task. A newspaper article reported: "In five days he's had three hours sleep. He shoved his glasses up on his sunburned forehead and dug his balled fists into burning eyes. 'It's got to come up pretty fast to beat us now,' he said. 'Let 'em keep up their end. We'll keep up ours [underlining in original].'"[396] Irene described how "he knew just how to place the sand bags—just where to look for the soft spots where seepage from the high water might break through."[397]

Mattie Kelleher was just as much of a community booster as was her husband. As well as being active in the Ridgedale Community Club, she was a member of the Women's Institute (WI), a provincial organization that brought local women together on a regular basis.[398] A neighbour who was also in the WI recalled how once, "when the ladies wished to leave and had to inform the driver of their coach, a hay wagon and team,

Mrs. Kelleher said 'I have rubber boots on' and she ran to the barn to bring the conveyance out." Overall, the respect that Mattie and Cornie gained in the community was sincere but may always have remained a bit circumspect, as suggested by a query made about them in their old age: "At our last Pioneers' gathering a friend said to me, 'Who is that couple over there? Nearly everyone who passes them stops to shake hands.'" [399]

SOCIALIZING WITH SCHOOLMATES

Very important to the Kellehers' way of life was sociability with others with whom they were comfortable. During the winter months, the Kellehers and their friends and neighbours enjoyed frequent Saturday night "coffee" dances at each others' houses. The furniture would be cleared out of the front room, powder scattered on the floor, and the music would begin. Someone would play a violin, someone else a guitar, and someone would call the quadrilles. The New Year's dance would always take place at the Kellehers' house. [400]

During the summer when the mosquitoes were bad, the Kellehers used their tug to take neighbours for picnics on Sumas Lake. [401] Irene recalled, "What lovely times were had on Kennedy's Ridge, swimming and playing on the sandy beach. All before the lake was drained." [402]

It was these relationships that gave depth and texture to the Kellehers' life together. Many people were entertained on the homestead as a matter of course in connection with Mattie's sewing or other aspects of their working lives, but when it came to friends who visited back and forth, they were more likely to share similar backgrounds and formative experiences. As Irene explained to me about a person whose name on a list she did not recognize, she "must have been part-Native because Mother visited with her." [403] Among the visitors was Mary Ann Purcell Holt, who as a young woman had been kept from marrying Cornelius in favour of a white man selected for her by her father. Particularly during the Kellehers' later years, she was frequently there, perhaps to talk about "old times," Irene mused to me. [404]

Many of the Kellehers' friends went back to their earliest childhoods. Cornie remained friendly with "old man Deroche."[405] The tie to
his godfather, whose wife, Marie, was Mattie's godmother as well as his
own, was the longest friendship the couple had. They saw beyond what
a child arrived from Ontario in 1890 recalled as a "hard, tough character"
with "long pointed whiskers" who was as "crabby as they make 'em."
Yet even this newcomer emphasized that Joe Deroche had a good side,
for "when we first came there, if they killed a pig they would give us
a big hunk of pork." Never losing a strong French-Canadian accent, he
was, very importantly, a survivor, being "a man of powerful physique and
indomitable perseverance."[406] In 1878, Deroche acquired a second 160
acres in anticipation of the Canadian Pacific Railway passing nearby.[407] It
did so, and Nicomen Station became the Deroches' northern boundary.
The family was sufficiently affluent to employ a Chinese servant, who at
the turn of the century received $150 a year, and for two sons to marry
white or almost white women.[408]

However much an illiterate Quebecer might have achieved worldly
success, he and his family remained, in Irene's useful phrase, "our kind."
Just as with the Kellehers, the Deroche family could never quite escape
British Columbia's culture of racism, which looked for evidence of failure
and then used it to justify differential attitudes and treatment. A memoir by a member of a local pioneer family took pains to point out, a bit
erroneously, that "Mr. and Mrs. Deroche were ¼ breeds," and went on to
describe their everyday lives in ways that implied surprise for any good
qualities the family might have possessed: "There was always a spittoon,
the old man had always a wad of chewing tobacco in his mouth and he
used to spit in the spittoon, it was made of brass.... Old Mr. Deroche was
very clean.... I do not know where they slept but no doubt they had several
rooms." The next paragraph made the author's biases even more visible:

> There were quite a few half breeds around in the olden days,
> but sad to say so many got drowned. A boat load would go
> off to Chilliwack and get liquor and get drunk and on the

way back would fall overboard and drown, then those left
would have a Potlatch. They all gathered at one house and
had a real party, lots of food etc, next day a funeral.[409]

The Kellehers' schoolmates were, like the Deroche family, "our kind." The star pupil of the generation just older than Cornelius was Charles Gardner. Shortly after wedding Mary Ellen Edwards, he "made his first break from the Mission" by leaving the position given him by the Oblates on his marriage in order to repair bridges on the Cariboo Wagon Road that had been taken out by high water during the spring. It did not prove easy for Charlie to support his growing family and, while pre-empting land at Dewdney, he got work in the spring of 1886 planking Vancouver's Hastings Street and then clearing land there, earning $2.25 a day and board.[410]

About this time, Charles's wife, Mary Ellen Edwards, fell ill. Her sister-in-law, Josephine Humphreys, recalled how in the summer of 1886 she went every day to take care of her and their three children, even though "I had to be at home nights, cow and hens to see to." By the next spring, Mary Ellen was so badly off that Josephine took her home to live with them. "She was very ill from [a] neglected cold, [and] her two young children died from whooping cough both within a day or two, a double funeral on May 28, 1887. I had her come to me where she passed." Josephine then took in Mary Ellen's son, seven-year-old Joe Gardner, until his father could recover from the triple blow.[411]

A child had to have a mother, and Charlie Gardner had soon found one for his son in sixteen-year-old Elvira Jane Garner. Her father, Robert Garner, like Charlie's, had arrived with the US boundary commission.[412] Robert had stayed true to his wife, Alice Joseph, daughter of the chief at Squah near Chilliwack, whom he married in a Methodist ceremony in 1869, disowned for doing so by his family back home in Kansas.[413] According to a descendant, the family gave him notice not to come home, so that even to the present day, there is virtually no contact with family members in the United States.

Son of a United States army lieutenant heading a commission surveying the boundary with British Columbia and of a Fraser Valley chief's daughter named Selaamia, Charles Gardner never met his father, who arranged for his protection, leading to his attending St. Mary's Mission alongside Cornie Kelleher and possibly to his having a family with Elvira Jane Garner, the daughter of another boundary official, who had, in contrast to Charles's father, stayed true to the Indigenous woman in his life and was disowned for doing so by his family in Kansas. Mission Community Archives, MCA-265-043

Garner ran the post office, which may be how Gardner got to know his second wife, or it may have been due to Elvira Jane's attendance at St. Mary's Mission girls' school.[414] It was only after Gardner stumbled once again, by trading his Dewdney property for a hapless Chilliwack livery stable, that he found a permanent occupation, running riverboats both on the Fraser River and in the north both during the Klondike gold rush of the late nineteenth century and after.[415]

By the time the Kellehers wed in 1898, Charlie had become Captain Gardner and was the most prominent among their schoolmates.[416] His occupation as a boat captain was one of the most lucrative open to a person of Indigenous descent. In 1901, he reported an annual income of $1,500 for having worked just seven months of the previous year, at a time when a good yearly wage was a third that amount.[417] He had to have experienced a certain ambivalence from time to time, given the attitudes

Over the course of time Charles Gardner became a very prestigious Captain Gardner, having charge of riverboats on the Fraser River and in the north during the Klondike gold rush, becoming thereby the most prominent among St. Mary's Mission pupils. Mission Community Archives, MCA-319-029

of the day. As pointed out proudly in a 1908 description of the *Beaver*, which he was then running thrice weekly between Chilliwack and New Westminster:

> The large dining room was shortened to give space for a second-class cabin for Chinese and Siwash passengers.... The ladies' saloon is at the rear of the boat upon the upper deck and is carpeted and upholstered with plush. The gentlemen's cabin and smoking room is in front and upholstered in leather.[418]

Given the common use of the contemptuous term "Siwash" to describe passengers of Indigenous descent, Captain Gardner may well have mused from time to time about where he himself belonged. Others never allowed him to escape the facts of his birth, as attested in an oral recollection by a long-time Mission resident as to how "Capt. Gardener was ½ Indian, he worked on the boats to Arctic," and "the Gardners were half breeds."[419]

Among the Kellehers' other schoolmates, now friends, were the Baker siblings. Alonzo Baker and Ellen Lacroix were, almost certainly with the same encouragement given to the three fatherless Edwards children and others, married to each other at the mission at the end of December 1884, aged nineteen and seventeen respectively.[420] There was an ongoing link between the families. Irene recalled how, when we were "just little children," there were boat excursions. "I can remember Mother getting us ready and, for part of the time, there'd be some dancing, and Alonzo would be playing the violin."[421]

Mattie kept in touch with Alonzo Baker's younger sister, Florence, her contemporary at the mission. They visited back and forth during the years Mattie lived at home with her father and later, when Flo worked for a time at the Royal City Hotel in New Westminster. It was almost certainly through her good offices that the Kellehers acquired a set of dining chairs from the hotel that Irene would still be using in 1998.[422] It was on these elegant Royal City Hotel chairs that Irene and I sat during our mornings together drinking Irene's meticulously prepared coffee along with a snack, usually also of her making.

AN ENDURING FRIENDSHIP WITH JOSEPHINE

Among the Kellehers' closest friends were the Edwards brothers, Pat and Henry, and their families, who lived just north of the Wellses' pre-emption. Cornie had gone to school with Pat, and Mattie with his wife, Josephine Humphreys, and likely also with Henry's wife, Fanny Cunning-ham.[423] As explained by Irene: "Well, all those people were you know, school girls, and all the same age. So they all visited, they were close friends, but not related."[424] Josephine's granddaughter Rosemarie, whom Josephine raised, explained to me how the friendship with Mattie went back to their being "pals" while at the mission.[425]

Josephine's character comes to the fore as a foster mother. In the late 1920s, Pat and Josephine Edwards took in a motherless orphan named Bernice Gerard, whose published memoir speaks to Josephine's generosity of spirit respecting their charge's neediness. The fisherman's wife who had adopted Bernice at birth and died when she was "scarcely two years old" was, in her memory, "a full-blooded Indian woman" for whom the small child longed.[426] A deteriorating home situation with Bernice's adoptive father and his four grown sons, all with "jet black hair and dark, swarthy skin; due of course to their French-Indian back-ground," caused the towheaded Bernice to be taken in over a summer by the Humphreys.[427]

Josephine stood in for the maternal support that had eluded Bernice Gerard. When an Edwards grandchild reminded her that "she's not *your* [italics in original] Grandma," she had gone to Josephine to be told that "she loved me just as much as if I were a real Indian like the rest." From Bernice's perspective as a white outsider when she published her memoir, by then a well-known evangelist preacher and former Vancouver city councillor, Josephine signified both what Bernice saw and wanted to see. "Even now that wonderful Indian woman, Josephine Edwards, lives in memory as my Grandma; certainly I never had another.

I remember her as beautiful when I was a preschooler.... It was she who sent me off to my first day of school with an apple in my hand for the teacher."[428]

The qualities Bernice Gerard attributed to Josephine were compatible with her being solely Indigenous, such as her "knowledge about which fungi were mushrooms and which were toadstools, what greens growing wild could be eaten, and what medicine could be found in the wilds." While living with Josephine and her family, "we regularly ate wild watercress, and dandelion greens, and once, I remember, the lot of us picking flowers for dandelion wine."[429] For this small child there was also discipline, for "Grandma believed in corporal punishment," but applied it in a fashion not incompatible, in Bernice's view, with traditional Indigenous practices.[430] "She proceeded carefully to see that the punishment suited the crime... until at last the bodily punishment that fell from her loving hand was almost nothing as measured against the heavy lessons she handed out."[431]

Another reason Bernice Gerard evoked the Edwards family solely within an "Indian" framework was that both Josephine and Pat had been "among the first students at the Roman Catholic Indian Mission School," whose student body had, by the time Bernice's memoir was published in 1988, long since become wholly Indigenous.[432] Not only that, but the Edwardses were not rich. "At the time Grandma took me in, her husband Pat was piecing together a living by fishing and mixed farming, the best part of which was his acres of raspberry bushes." To help out, "Grandma was a good flower and vegetable gardener, and I was her eager-beaver helper.... Digging up the ground for the first time around, or hoeing, or raking or even weeding was good if Grandma and I could talk as we worked, and she would hand out a little praise to her husky digger."[433]

Bernice Gerard described activities in which the Kellehers may have shared. "At the Edwards' family, a good part of living was the pleasure of watching so many people come and go. Besides Grandma's sons and daughters and grandchildren, there were regular visitors from Harrison Lake and Chemainus [where an otherwise unidentified "Uncle" and "Auntie" lived]. In the berry season, pickers and helpers ate in a common dining room."[434]

Such a perspective did not alter in Bernice Gerard's depiction of Josephine in old age, although she was not quite as elderly as she seemed in her one-time charge's imagination. "At over one hundred years of age, still possessed of classic features, she was proudly a representative of her own people. It took years for me to understand why she often said to her children, 'We are proud to be Indian.'"[435]

This outsider perspective, grounded in a larger society that had largely written out persons living between Indigenous and white except in derogatory ways, complemented how Josephine was viewed by "our kind." Throughout the long friendship

Josephine Humphreys Edwards' long life of service to Fraser Valley families and to others in time of need, including future Vancouver city councillor and preacher Bernice Gerard, caused her always to stand a little apart from her contemporaries, still so in this photograph of her at ninety-two years of age in 1958. Mission Community Archives, MCA-GPC-028-028

between the Edwards family and the Kellehers, Josephine always stood a bit apart, acknowledged as having a superior white lineage, even if it had to be enjoyed in the shadows. Perhaps it was Josephine's extended schooling, perhaps her father's political career that caused her to be known sometimes as "Mrs. Pat," but at others, as "Madame Josephine," as Irene named her in our conversations.[436] Publicly, Thomas Basil Humphreys the politician had no daughter Josephine once she was dispatched to the mission. On his death in 1890, his occupation was given as "gentleman," a world away from Josephine's everyday life in the Fraser Valley, his children only those who were wholly white.[437]

Privately, the situation between Josephine and her father was more complex, just as it was for similar families across British Columbia during these years when so many newcomers traded in Indigenous for white wives in order to improve their chances of acquiring a stake in the dominant society. Father and daughter remained in touch until his death in 1890, although her letters were far more frequent than his.[438]

While Josephine also kept in contact with her mother, Chehalis chief's daughter, Lucy Semo, it was her father for whom she longed. Almost two-thirds of a century after his death, Josephine copied out in her own hand pieces of the many obituaries of Thomas Basil Humphreys containing such phrases as "a generous friend, sympathetic and kind-hearted," "one of the most widely known public men in British Columbia," "his marvelous talent for public speaking," "a brilliant talker... possessing a clear, well modulated voice, a marvelous command of language and a comprehensive knowledge of public affairs," "he seldom wounded unnecessarily the feeling of those whose public conduct he assailed," and "had not a personal enemy in the province."[439] Whether or not Josephine kept in touch with her white half-siblings after her father's death, her handwritten memoir of the early 1950s contained two Victoria addresses and a telephone number.[440]

Perhaps in part because Mattie Kelleher always felt a slight sense of competition with "Madame Josephine," she determined to become, on her model, a good hostess. "People always enjoyed the hospitality of her home, her guests felt comfortable in her presence and she was a perfect cook."[441] A friend remembered "her lovely friendly smile when he visited the homestead and her bountiful hospitality." According to Irene, "making a tasty meal was an inborn ability for my mother," and "she loved to try out something new, a cake, or cookies, or something she fancies."[442] Irene recalled how "she was frequently complimented on her chicken dinners and apple pies."[443] Not only that, "she collected recipes by the hundreds and also dress patterns."[444] Such sociability extended to Mattie's sewing. A woman who took her sewing to her for many years recalled how "a slice of Mrs. Kelleher's home-made bread is much enjoyed."[445]

While visiting Josephine's granddaughter Rosemarie George with Irene, we had tea in her grandmother's flowered English cups and saucers.[446] In like manner, a highlight of Mattie's hospitality was "the lovely friendly cups of tea she quietly prepared for her guests."[447] Rosemarie recalled Mattie sitting down and having tea every afternoon in delicate cups and saucers. "I guess that was the English in her."[448]

In this respect, Mattie may have upstaged Josephine, for, if very fortunate, her guests would drink tea not out of just any china cups and saucers but from those issued to commemorate events in the British royal family, whose lives Mattie followed closely.[449] Irene took pride in how her mother was a tiny, fine-boned woman with the delicate china very much in character.[450] Mattie's special treasure was two cups and saucers purchased to honour King George VI's visit to Canada in 1939 and Queen Elizabeth's coronation in 1953.

I glimpsed this aspect of Irene's inheritance the first day we spent together. On leaving, I jotted in my notes how Irene had "provided coffee at about 11:15, the table having been all set with royal coffee sets and two buns (which she apologized for having made the day before), a glass dish with a square of butter and a glass jar of clear jam (which she made and combined apple with raspberry for colour)."[451] Responding to Irene's curiosity about my suitably British-born husband, on a Sunday morning the next spring I brought him along to meet her, which again brought out the royal sets.[452] At the end of a much later visit by myself, I was humbled when Irene insisted that I have the prized cups and saucers as my own as a remembrance of Irene and her family. They sit proudly in our living room.

FAMILY MATTERS

It was not just friends and neighbours who occupied the Kellehers during their many years together. Although Cornelius ended up an only child without an immediate family, he did have one or more relatives whom he saw from time to time. Among visitors to the homestead were the Cheers of Whonnock, who, Irene told me, were related to her Wells

grandmother, Madeleine. "They used to visit Mom and Dad."[453] Among
the children of Daniel Cheer, described in the 1891 census as Hawai-
ian-born and a fisherman, and of an Indigenous woman named Mary
was Henry, born in about 1879. Henry had also attended St. Mary's and
in adulthood lived, according to a white neighbour, on the Stave River
Reserve near Whonnock.[454] Harry's and Cornie's similar schooling may
have solidified the link between them.

If Cornie's relatives were scarce, Mattie had enough to occupy both
of them. The life courses of her one sister and five brothers exemplify
the challenges that sons of mixed descent faced in a changing British
Columbia. The skills her brothers acquired as a farmer's sons counted
for little without the literacy and numerical skills formal schooling gave
so as to accommodate to the dominant society, where they were in any
case at a disadvantage. Mattie and Sarah Jane found partners of similar
mixed descent, but a still uneven sex ratio made it more difficult for sons
to do so, especially if they lacked economic stability. Landholding was an
important asset, making it possible for a family to be largely self-sufficient in the everyday where all else failed. Without land, the alternative
for many men was a life on the margins, living from pillar to post, which
was precisely what the five Wells brothers did for the most part.

Mattie's sister, Sarah Jane, had a still ambitious, if not necessarily
reliable, husband in Gabe Lacroix. A few years after the tumultuous first
trip north, they homesteaded so far north "it was too cold for their stock,"
and then at Round Lake near Telkwa in northwestern British Columbia,
whence his younger brother Joe soon followed.[455] Having no children of
her own, Sarah Jane brought up Joe's daughter and two sons after his wife
died.[456] At the time of the 1901 census, Gabriel Lacroix described himself
as a storekeeper in the Hazelton area, with an annual income of $500.
Their household included their niece Emily, born in 1896 in Hazelton of
French and Babine descent.[457] At the time of Gabriel Lacroix's death in
May 1933, the couple was living at "Hubert near Telkwa."[458] Four years
later, Sarah Jane, then aged seventy-four, came to live with the Kellehers
on their homestead, where she died a dozen years later in 1949.[459]

Mattie's oldest brother, Joshua Wells, never found himself. He had no children and was by disposition, according to his niece Irene, a "regular hermit."[460] In about 1886, on reaching the necessary legal age of twenty-one, he took up a homestead adjoining his father's.[461] Losing it, Joshua worked in the area. When the railway was coming through, he graded, using oxen.[462] When some new settlers wanted to build "a great big house, great big kitchen and bedrooms all along the side of it," Joshua "hauled all the lumber."[463] He took on the Wells family homestead on his father's death in 1898, but was more interested in selling off parcels of it than in farming it.

> Uncle Josh had a <u>lot</u> [emphasis in original] of land. In the history of Hatzic, everyone bought from Uncle Josh. Well, originally it started out to be a sale. Whether there was any money, I know there was a lot of handshakes. A lot of people say so-and-so bought land from Josh Wells. And it was done on a handshake because he always said if the signature was no good, you know.... There was no thing better than a handshake. Because if they're not going to pay, they are not going to pay.[464]

However good or bad handshakes were as a means of disposing of the Wells homestead, in less than a decade Joshua had "lost it through bad deals and management." As explained by Irene: "Uncle Josh would buy something or do something and didn't pay for it, well then he lost everything. They didn't have a thing."[465] So he moved on. "After he lost his property in Hatzic he lived at Wade's Landing for a few years" and then at Sumas Prairie.[466] An acquaintance recalled his "little boat," "almost like a canoe, or a rowboat," that "had two posts" and "this cute little serrated fringe on the top."[467] Even though he never went to school, he was always buying books and perhaps, to an extent, used them to escape a sometimes harsh reality.[468] When Joshua Wells became ill, it was Cornelius who "took him to the Abbotsford Hospital," where he died in 1947.[469]

The next of the Wells sons, Chester, did not have much of an adulthood. He worked around home and then at New Westminster. There in 1904, still a young man, he was "accidentally killed while discharging coal by being struck with [a] descending coal box."[470]

Then came Jim, who as a young man had gone north with his sisters, Sarah Jane and Mattie. "He wanted to go up there all the time, so he went back."[471] Mostly a prospector hoping to strike it rich, Jim also worked as a mine recorder and fishing inspector based at Kitselas on the Skeena River and, when the Grand Trunk Railway was constructed, at Usk, which was brought into being by the rail line.[472] "The Indian women would get after him for spoiling their fishnet and take him and throw him in the river.... They wanted to fish like they used to fish, and I guess they were being restricted."[473] At some point, Jim ended up in jail and his brother-in-law Cornelius Kelleher "had to sell cattle to bail him out."[474]

Jim remained in contact with his sister Sarah Jane, who had settled at Round Lake, and at one point, according to their niece Irene, "had a child by a lady working for Auntie."[475] Jim's daughter with a woman Irene recalled as Selina was Mary, whose daughter Gloria would visit Irene in Abbotsford from time to time.[476] Jim drowned in the Skeena River on a wintry Christmas Eve in 1926 while attempting to cross the river at Usk by rowboat.[477]

Mattie's next older brother, Amos, was equally restless. A man born in the Fraser Valley in the late nineteenth century recalled: "Amos and [his brother] Joshua used to run the supplies in on the tugs when the water was up. They used to bring the stuff up to the camps and then collect the milk from the farmers and take it down."[478] In late summer of 1896, twenty-three-year-old Amos got his sister's good friend Josephine Edwards pregnant. She was a decade his senior and had at that time five sons between the ages of two and nine.[479] Born May 12, 1897, their daughter was named Lucy after Josie's mother, and she was raised by Josie and her husband as their own.[480] It would be Lucy's daughter Rosemarie who would share Josephine's story and her writings with me, making it possible to tell her remarkable story.[481] Sometime thereafter,

Among Irene Kelleher's Wells uncles, her most beloved, depicted here shooting ducks on Sumas Lake, was Andrew, admired for his violin playing, assistance to her father in building the homestead, and for his good manners. *Mission Community Archives, MCA-GPC018-0035*

Amos headed north as had his older siblings, Jim and Sarah Jane. He took up land not far from Sarah Jane at Round Lake near Telkwa, while also working on pack trains.[482] In his mid-forties, in 1917, Amos married the nineteen-year-old daughter of a local labourer in an Anglican ceremony at Sarah Jane's home. They had three children.[483]

The youngest of Mattie's brothers, Andrew—beloved by Irene for his violin playing—never settled down.[484] As well as attending the local schools at Dewdney and Mission, he spent a few months at the large Coqualeetza Indian residential school at Sardis, which accepted him based on his mother's Indigenous descent. According to its register, he entered the first grade on December 6, 1893, when he was already sixteen years old, and left on June 27, 1894, then in the second grade, with no further information supplied.[485] It was perhaps there that Andrew was taught the manners he kept through a lifetime, such as always walking, according to Irene, on the outside with a woman.[486] Andrew learned to play the violin and was "much in demand at the dances as the music was supplied by local talent." Irene recalled how "he seemed to be able to produce music from his violin that made a thrill go through one's body."[487] All her life, Irene was enthralled by his talent.

In his work life, Andrew did a bit of this and a bit of that. Coqualeetza tracked its supposedly Indigenous charges after they left the school and noted after his entry only that he "has been following the calling of a fisherman," but "particulars of his life not known."[488] According to Irene, "he was clever with machinery and tools," "built a few boats in his time," and "worked at various jobs," including "logging camps up the coast of British Columbia and Kingcome Inlet and other places on the coast [and] at Sedro-Woolley in Washington State." Andrew enlisted in the First World War together with Pat and Josephine Edwards' son Art and went overseas to France.[489]

Earlier Andrew had helped Cornelius build his house and, in turn, Cornie gave Andrew forty acres from the homestead as a base from which, after returning home from the war, he "spent many years fishing on the Fraser River" with "his own gear and boat and living in a boat house."[490] Family mattered. When his older brother Jim drowned in 1926, Andrew sold his fishing gear and boat to get the money to go north to locate his body and did in fact find it in time for a spring burial.[491] Andrew married late in life and died in 1954.[492]

LIVING BETWEEN INDIGENOUS AND WHITE

It was not just the trials and tribulations of Mattie's brothers but everyday life that reminded the Kellehers and their friends and neighbours of the full extent to which they perforce made their way between Indigenous and white. Cornie repeatedly held his ground, accommodating to numerous interviewers whose questions seemed intended to diminish his family, if not directly, then by inference:

> Wells: What nationality is your family?
>
> Kelleher: They're Irishmen, County Cork, Ireland.
>
> Wells: Good. And he married an Indian?
>
> Kelleher: Indian woman, yes.
>
> Wells: Indian woman. And what was her name?

The interviewer, Oliver Wells, referred to the Kellehers and their daughter, Irene, as "informants." A note on the back of the resulting publication described them as "Native friends."[493]

Quietly and privately, both Cornie and Mattie kept in touch with their mothers' families. Cornie recovered contact after leaving school. His uncle would come and visit and talk in his own language so that Cornie learned or possibly relearned it.[494] According to Irene, referring to St. Mary's school where he spent his childhood and youth, "having been told he couldn't use his mother's tongue, but yet he retained that language from that time on."[495] Cornelius also got to know his maternal grandfather. "I can remember some of the stories of my Grandfather Job—stories [that go] as far back as his grandfather's time."[496] Cornie recalled how:

> My Indian grandfather used to come over and tell me—you know, he used to come over and stay with me—long before I was married, you know—and tell me yarns.... They used to come over from Nooksack and camp over in Hatzic Island.... There was a great place for great, big cedars and they would make canoes in the wintertime. The young bucks could get way up into the mountains there and get goat wool to make their blankets, and meat too.... My grandfather used to tell me how they caught the deer. He said: "I used to go and get a sweat bath." They'd make a sweat bath of rocks into a cave on the side of the bank, in order to take the human scent off themselves... and they'd shoot them. Then he said the women folks would come and pack them—skin them and take their sinews to sew, our buckskin and all that sort of thing.[497]

Cornie told a story about Mount Baker, which gave off smoke at some point when he was in school, likely in 1879.[498] "My grandfather used to talk about it. He said that's where they first got their fire to cook with." Cornelius developed a certain respect for Indigenous practices, for example, "those Indian doctors, some of them were good." Each spring Cornie made remedies from dock leaves and other plants, a practice that likely had an Indigenous origin through his mother's family.[499]

Despite the departure of Mattie's mother, Ki-ka-twa, also known as Julia, when she was an infant, Mattie also kept in touch with her mother's family and recalled:

> My mother's father, who was christened Peter, sometimes came down from Pt. Douglas and told very interesting stories to the family in his native tongue which I could not understand but, of course, learned much of his tales. One was of a small pox epidemic which swept through the area in the long ago killing many Indians. One night grandfather had a dream in which he was told to put cedar boughs about the house as a protection against the disease. This he did, and the whole family escaped infection. For a time the old gentleman worked in New Westminster. He passed away in the late 1880s.[500]

What is remarkable in retrospect is that Mattie's mother returned to the family she had long since left. Irene told how "my dad built a little house there [near Hatzic] for Grandmother Wells and that is where she lived till she died [in 1906]."[501] Everyday life was, in other words, much more complicated than outward appearances might suggest, this during a time period in British Columbia when such relationships were to be eschewed in the interests of everyday survival even at the edges of the dominant society.

It seems fair to say that the Kellehers did not overly emphasize their Indigenous roots, nor did they deliberately obscure them. Irene twice reflected to me about her father that, overall, "he was more Indian than white."[502] Within this context, he sat "on many local committees dealing with Indian problems and issues."[503] At the same time, in his numerous interviews, Cornie Kelleher never identified himself with Indigenous persons, who from his years in residential school he always described as "they," saying, for example, "they made their own nets," and so forth. In similar fashion, he once recalled about his early years: "There were a lot of Indians them days—not like now, you'd see one fellow now and then—a man. But there were thousands of them here."[504]

To the extent that a gentle obfuscation occurred, it was sometimes deliberate, other times at the behest of others concerned to "protect" the couple at a time when a culture of racism still persisted across British Columbia and beyond. Thus, in a lengthy biographical article of 1950 about Cornelius Kelleher based on an interview with him, his mother was described only as a "girl" and his mother-in-law was given as having a father and no mother at all.[505] Similarly, when Mattie and then Cornie Kelleher died in the late 1960s, their daughter, Irene, gave their "racial origin" in both cases as white.[506]

Perhaps the most astute comment respecting the lived experience of this clutch of Fraser Valley families belongs to Josephine Humphreys Edwards, who in the course of writing her pithy memoir, shared with me by her granddaughter, had "quite a long time to remember, pleasant and otherwise, but mostly pleasant."[507] Much as with her good friend Josephine, a neighbour recalled about Mattie Kelleher how she "never complained of hardships or heavy loads or the tragedies of life."[508] Mattie, Cornie, and their schoolmates witnessed generations of change. They each coped and accommodated as best they could, although Cornie sometimes longed for an earlier day. "My dad used to say it was getting too crowded."[509]

WINDING DOWN

Apart from leaving their mountain homestead for three or four years in the early 1920s to help their son Albert make a go of his parents' old farm, the Kellehers' everyday life went on relatively unchanged from their marriage in 1898 until 1943, when their house was destroyed by fire.[510] Mattie was away at Mission and walking back up the mountain when Cornie met her to tell her that everything had been lost. With the help of neighbours, they rebuilt higher up the mountain with an even better view over the valley.[511] Life went on much as it had before so

Cornelius and Julia Kelleher were recognized for their understanding of Fraser Valley history; this photograph was taken in 1963 about the time Imbert Orchard of the CBC interviewed them in depth. Mission Community Archives, 0025-MCA334-060

that when Imbert Orchard made several trips to the homestead in March 1963 to interview the Kellehers as "pioneers," he was always invited to stay for supper.[512]

Then came the winter of 1964–65, which Irene, who had retired from teaching only the previous spring, described as "just terrible."[513] Aged ninety-two and eighty-eight, the Kellehers left their homestead for good on December 19, 1964, to move in with their unmarried daughter, by then living in Abbotsford.[514] Irene had played a growing role in their care, so her mother noted in 1957: "Irene comes up regularly in her jeep, which she keeps at the foot of the hill and takes us down in it. Then we go in her car shopping and visiting or just for a drive."[515] The couple spent several more years together. Mattie died on January 13, 1967, at age ninety-one, Cornie on November 12, 1969, at age ninety-seven.[516]

IRENE ALONE

And so we come to Irene alone.

By the time of Cornie and Mattie Kelleher's deaths, their children were already well past middle age. While their lives had largely been formed in the shadow of their parents' generation, Albert and Irene had also learned from their own experiences and struck out in new directions. There was an important difference between parents and children. Whereas Cornie and Mattie were by descent "half-breeds," Albert and Irene were doubly so because both parents had a white and an Indigenous parent. They did not have that double experience as children, but were "half-breeds" within a "half-breed" setting from the moment of their births. A consequence is that they may have experienced more strongly the force of discrimination still rampant against persons of mixed descent and perhaps internalized more deeply the inferiority that others attached to them.

ALBERT GOING HIS OWN WAY

Born in 1900, Albert was the Kellehers' oldest child to survive infancy. As explained by his younger sister, Irene, he may have been put off schooling by a bad experience. She recalled the year when "everybody failed... the whole school."[517] He left school at age seventeen, whereupon he worked dredging gravel and cutting shingle bolts before beginning to farm on his parents' earlier property in 1920. Increasingly he was, like his father, involved in the larger community. In 1944, he became secretary-treasurer of a newly formed Ridgedale Credit Union, a position he held until 1952. In 1940, Albert married Daisy Moore, with whom he had two sons. When they became interested in 4-H, their father became an assistant leader of a Jersey Calf Club. In 1959, Albert Kelleher sold the Kelleher family farm and the next year moved to Abbotsford.[518] He died on December 22, 1987.[519]

What is clear from my conversations with Irene is that she and Albert and then his family were not close, at least not from Irene's perspective. They were not family, certainly not in the way that Irene's mother had all her life kept tabs on her siblings.

IRENE'S MODEST AMBITION

In contrast to Albert, who left school before graduating, his younger sister persisted. Irene passed her provincial entrance examinations and moved on to Matsqui High School, where she initially worked in exchange for her board.[520] "But when I failed my last year, Junior Matriculation, I continued high school from my parents' homestead on Sumas Mountain."[521] In fact, everyone failed their exams that year, so she did not feel that badly about it.[522]

In high school, Irene had a favourite teacher who encouraged her to be the best she could be. "Her image must have stayed with me because from that time on, I wanted to be a teacher."[523] As a consequence, Irene continued on to the provincial normal school in Vancouver, which was then the post-secondary route to becoming a public school teacher.[524] Her mother arranged for her to board with the family of a railway section foreman whom the Kellehers knew.[525]

Irene repeatedly pointed out during our conversations how her year in normal school, 1920–21, was in no way ordinary or straightforward. When she told me "there were only two of us at normal," she was not referring to the size of her class, but to her distinctive position in it.[526] There was only "one other person who was Native and she was from North Vancouver," but Irene never found out precisely who it was among her 150 or so fellow students, of whom all but 9 were women.[527] "Someone said there was one other."[528] In part for that reason, Irene quickly figured out she was more likely to succeed by merging into the background than by putting herself forward and thereby being found out. Not without reason, Irene's entry in the class yearbook has under it the poem "The tongue should stay behind the teeth. He who talks much talks to no effect."[529] The unintended consequence of Irene's self-protection strategy was that she "failed" her year at normal school due to what she remembered as "excessive shyness."[530]

Irene was nonetheless given a permit as a kind of field trial or second chance and, despite this setback, became a lifelong teacher.[531] While British Columbia's culture of racism did not deter her, there is no question but that it formed the direction and basis of her career. She was repeatedly slid into the edges of the edge, to the least desirable location—on the assumption that people in the locality were so grateful to have any teacher at all, they would not object to that person being of mixed descent. Interlocking prejudices worked against Irene: the assumptions of those assigning teachers to schools, their suppositions about what the assumptions in the localities would be, and then what those assumptions actually were. Each of these reasons, much less the trio acting together, worked against Irene, and yet she persevered.

TEACHING AT THE EDGES

Irene began with what might seem to have been a modest ambition, which was to return to the small school in her home community so that she could live at home and help sustain her parents, then in their mid- to late forties. Irene didn't stand a chance of doing so. Her hopes were bluntly and determinedly dashed. "When I left normal, I applied at Matsqui but I was turned down because they did not want a Native teacher of their children," as her father was told by someone on the local school board.[532] "I could not teach in the district. The secretary was an Englishman, he didn't want a half-breed teaching his children." And "we were half-breeds." To my protestation in that conversation that "half-breed" was not a nice word and perhaps should not be used in anything she wrote or I wrote on her behalf, Irene responded in no uncertain terms, this three-quarters of a century later: "Exactly so, but that's what we were. Half-breeds, that's what we were, and that's what we still are."[533]

Irene wrote letters to various places applying for jobs, the consequence a coincidence.[534] "After I got out of normal, my first school was up on the Skeena River, where my mother had gone many years ago. I taught at Usk for a couple of years."[535] By now her mother's brother, Uncle Jim, with whom Mattie had had her mighty adventure, lived nearby.

Jim was there to greet Irene on that summer day in 1921 when she stepped off the train at Usk, which was the only way to reach that remote logging and mining community located some 1,200 kilometres north of the Fraser Valley.[536] Although grateful for his presence, Irene may have all the same breathed a sigh of relief that, as she put it to me, "they didn't connect us."[537] Nor was the local community likely to do so, for Jim lived in what Irene described as a "shack" down by the river, whereas she boarded at the local hotel.[538] All the same, in Irene's memory, "they didn't expect what they saw, she's a half-breed."[539]

Irene survived her first year of teaching in what was just the two-room Usk School's third year of operation, and she was pleased to be invited back for a second year, 1922–23.[540] Miss I.J.M. Kelleher, as she was named in the annual provincial public schools report, taught thirty boys and girls roughly divided between the beginning three levels of first primer, second primer, and first reader, for which she received an annual salary of $1,050.[541]

Teachers were assessed by a visiting school inspector who would arrive unexpectedly, and Irene did well. "I guess Mr. Fraser, the inspector, must have thought I was capable because at the end of the two years, he granted me my permanent teaching certificate. It was a second-class certificate but it meant I could teach."[542] The level of a certificate related to the range of courses a person was qualified to teach.

Irene took special pride that she kept none of her teacher's salary for herself, apart from necessary expenses, and repaid her parents all the money they had provided to make it possible for her to go to normal school.[543] Perhaps it was to economize that, during her second year, she did not go home for Christmas, but spent the holidays with her aunt, Sarah Jane Lacroix, and her family, who were homesteading at Round Lake about 200 kilometres to the east. There she also visited with Chrissie Allard, one of the many persons with whom the family home had been shared during Irene's childhood.[544] Irene's principal expense on herself, so far as I could determine, comprised photographs of her students, their schools, and her faraway family that she took and carefully placed in an album, which she took great pride in sharing with me as we talked.[545]

Irene kept on teaching at the most remote locations to which a young woman could possibly be sent. "After Usk, I taught at Doreen... an overnight mining town with a one-room school. Then, I taught on Hunter Island (off Bella Bella)."[546] Doreen, where Irene spent the 1923–24 school year, was a divisional point between Smithers and Terrace on the rail line running by Usk. Irene boarded with a family, and while she was there, a fight broke out between the parents and the trustees. In the end, the schoolhouse was locked up, forcing her to find another posting for the upcoming school year of 1924–25.

To get to Hunter Island, where Irene was dispatched, proved to be even more difficult than to Usk or Doreen, both on a rail line. Irene was picked up from the steamer running up the coast to Bella Bella, parallel to the southern tip of Haida Gwaii. She was met there by the local medical doctor, who took her the rest of the way in a small boat.[547] On Hunter Island, which had in Irene's memory "a very good school," she had her first experience teaching unfamiliar ethnic groups. It had been settled by Icelandic people, whose numbers were in decline.[548] The earliest had arrived in 1912 and the population peaked at about seventy individuals who made their living by fishing or logging.

There was a teacherage in which to live, and for the first time in her life, Irene was cast onto her own resources. "I had to batch and live in my own house, it rained and I cried; I did not know how to live by myself."[549] Over time Irene realized that, yes, she could do it.[550] For the first time she cooked for herself. "They had the cutest little stove, it was a regular stove and the oven was up there on top, in the chimney. Oh, it was good baking!" Groceries were sent by boat from Vancouver by Woodward's store, which was at that point in time a common means for persons in remote communities to get supplies.[551] Four children were from a single family, and every morning, when "the boatman rowed me across the bay to the school," Irene took two others with her.[552] One of them, underage, was needed to make up the minimum number of six necessary to keep the school open.[553]

The adventure that the north gave was all well and good, but most teachers Irene's age were retreating from the workplace into marriage. Repeatedly asked by me during our many conversations why she did not do so, Irene responded bluntly, "Nobody would have me."[554] In another conversation, not with me, Irene's response was similar. "Who would have wanted me? Nobody would have wanted me."[555] Another time, referring to herself in the third person, "she wasn't accepted."[556]

Irene did not share in the common practice of the day in British Columbia, whereby the newly arrived teacher was the belle of the ball at local dances, vigorously courted by men in need of wives. Irene's experience, at least in her memory, was the reverse. "I wasn't even invited to the dances at home."[557] When she did nonetheless attend, "they didn't ask me to dance; I was a half-breed, I didn't belong."[558]

Not only that, but by the time Irene was of marriageable age just after the First World War, the earlier shortage of newcomer women had moderated, due to major immigration before the war and to the loss of young men during the war. There were enough white women to go around. Irene recalled two beaus, but both situations ended badly. At Doreen she had a man paying attention to her but then his sister came to visit "from down the coast," took one look at Irene, saw her as an "Indian," and vetoed the relationship. The other time a man who had been courting her came to visit Irene's family while she was home on holidays and, according to Irene, her brother said such nasty things about her that she never heard from him again after he returned north.[559] "I used to cry a lot."[560]

It was likely the realization that teaching was to be a lifelong enterprise rather than a preliminary to marriage that prompted a courageous decision for any young woman, more so for one enmeshed within a culture of racism. During the academic year 1925–26, Irene went "to the University of British Columbia and got my first-class certificate from the newly opened university."[561] It was, in her recollection, UBC's "first year at Point Grey," and indeed it was.[562] To do this was not easy, she recalled, for there was always the sense of being set apart: "The year I spent at UBC I was the only half-breed there; there was only one other one at normal school." Irene first boarded at a house near the university that she located from a notice on a bulletin board. Later she lived with a family acquaintance farther away from the campus.[563] Perhaps in part for that reason she did not do as well as she might have hoped, having to repeat some exams and getting special coaching.[564] Yet she persevered through the year and, later, at the Victoria or Vancouver normal schools, would take "summer school courses" for over a third of a century, 1924 to 1958, to keep apace with the times.[565]

Irene was always very hopeful of being able to teach close enough to home to live with her parents, and for a time she almost made it. After UBC, Irene taught for a year, 1926–27, in the farming community of Flood, west of Hope, where she "had the whole thing."[566] If not near enough to live at home, the one-room school was the next best thing because Irene could take a local train home on weekends.[567] She proved to be a memorable teacher, being commended almost sixty years later in a local history of Flood as the teacher of the young son and daughter of a Swedish immigrant family.[568]

Irene then taught for three years, 1927–30, east of Abbotsford at Kilgard, home to a brick-making factory.[569] Perhaps Irene's mixed descent did play a role in her being offered the job, for, she explained, children considered to be Indians attended. Harry Kelly, whom Irene remembered as being from Port Douglas and at school with her father, had his own land and therefore was permitted to send his children to public school.[570] While at Kilgard, Irene would "drive there and back over the mountain from home, with her horse and two-wheeled cart."[571] Both of these Fraser Valley jobs were possible only because, Irene considered, they were in neighbouring school districts to where her parents lived.[572]

For all of their convenience, the jobs were fraught with difficulties. Irene took a day off from Kilgard to observe another school, as was common practice for teachers during these years, but someone "told on me." The school inspector—"they say he burnt up the road"—rushed to Kilgard to reprimand her.[573]

COMMITTING TO DOUKHOBOR CHILDREN

The perception of uneven treatment was perhaps somewhat easier for Irene to bear because, after a decade in the classroom, she was embarking on a new adventure putting her capacity as a teacher to the test.[574] As shared during our first conversation together, testifying to its importance in her life: "I guess that was the time I was getting ready for the Doukhobors."[575]

The impetus for Irene to take such an unexpected step lay, she explained to me, with Philip Sheffield, a career teacher married to a granddaughter of Billy Bristol. A New Yorker attracted west by the California and British Columbia gold rushes, Bristol was the long-time Fraser Valley mail carrier.[576] A white woman who arrived in British Columbia as a small child during the gold rush described admiringly in her memoir how "the express agent, Bill Bristol by name, we always looked upon as a great hero" for making "the trip from [New] Westminster every two weeks... with the mail."[577] Partnered with a woman described on their marriage certificate as "Mary (Indian)," Bristol was admired by Irene's parents.[578]

The Kellehers' respect for Bristol comes through in their responses to being queried by a white historian, "Do you know the Indian that was the mail carrier on the Sumas River?" Irene's mother replied, "I don't know about the Indian, but there's a fellow that carried the mail over the mountains," at which point her husband added just as pointedly, "Bill Bristol was the fellow that carried; he lived at Hope. He used to carry the mail from New Westminster up along there during the winter time,

The Kellehers' friendship with the family of long-time Fraser Valley mail carrier Billy Bristol, a New Yorker attracted by the gold rush and here photographed in about 1880, almost certainly encouraged Irene's positive response to his grandson-in-law's search for teachers of British Columbia's Doukhobor children, whose families were opposed on principle to their becoming literate and thereby to Irene teaching them, for almost a decade in sometimes dangerous conditions. Royal BC Museum and Archives, A-020022

along Yale Road; then he'd come across from the Mission there. They'd be always watching for him."[579] From the perspective of Irene's parents, Bristol was a fellow human being and a friend, as opposed to "the Indian."

Comfortable with Sheffield by virtue of her parents' respect for Bristol and his family, Irene responded to his commitment, as the provincial government's official trustee and therefore responsible for British Columbia's Doukhobor children, to secure for them especially trained teachers. In the summer of 1929, following her first year at Kilgard, Irene took a course at the Victoria normal school on "Teaching English to New Canadians" instructed by Sheffield, along with folk dancing and first aid. In summer 1930 she enrolled in an art course in leather work and in typewriting, speech training, and a second "Teaching English to New Canadians" course. The "New Canadians" courses were designed to be preparatory to teaching Doukhobor children.[580] The reason, Irene explained to me and as she found out, lay in a volatile situation making especially trained teachers essential.[581]

Coalescing in eighteenth-century Russia, Doukhobors perceived themselves as a community of the saved with God's presence residing in each self as opposed to salvation being sought external to the self, as in most religious faiths. Doukhobors' opposition to external authority over their chosen way of life had caused large numbers to depart Russia at the end of the nineteenth century, including 7,000 who moved to Saskatchewan on the promise of free land. Subsequent demands that homesteaded land be individually registered with an oath of allegiance taken to the Crown, thus acquiescing to external authority, caused 5,000 or more Doukhobors to move west to British Columbia. They did so subsequent to their spiritual leader purchasing large chunks of land in the West Kootenay and Boundary regions, which was then divided into hundred-acre plots.

Living communally in large houses with up to fifty people in each, Doukhobors recreated in British Columbia the austere, self-contained way of life they had known in Russia. The institution generating the most tension was the public school, viewed as assimilating children away from their culture. "Just as soon as the person reached read and write education, then within a short time leaves his parents and relations and undertakes unreturnable journey." The absence of a written holy book gave no meaning to literacy. "We adopt our children to learn at wide school of Eternal Nature."[582]

As official trustee, Sheffield sought to ameliorate the situation, hence the special classes Irene took. Provincial regulations requiring school attendance from age seven upwards continued to be met, all the same, with alternating semi-compliance and confrontation. Tactics from the spring of 1923 onwards included burning schools as a means of closing them down.

Irene began teaching Doukhobor children in the fall of 1930. To do so was a brave undertaking for anyone, even more so for a thirty-year-old woman on her own. Irene was dispatched to Glade, founded in 1911 on the Kootenay River between the communities of Castlegar and Nelson as one of eleven British Columbia Doukhobor communal villages and the second largest among them. Much like the others, Glade comprised two large wooden communal houses, a U-shaped outbuilding for animals, a common bathhouse, and a blacksmith shop. Glade also contained two brick buildings, one a general store, the other a school guarded against arsonists.[583] Despite her distinctive circumstances, Irene's annual salary of $1,020 differed not at all from what it had been a decade earlier when she began teaching. She was now responsible for thirty-three children divided between grades one, two, and three.

At the time of Irene's arrival by ferry, which was the only means in or out of Glade, its school was newly constructed, with classrooms on either end of a four-room teacherage, or living quarters, in the middle, located there for protection.[584] Regardless, "during my first Christmas there, someone threw blasting powder at the school.... I'll never forget the smell... and we spent the rest of the evening serving coffee to the policemen who came to protect us. The following spring when the parents started full-scale terrorist activities, the children were taken away and boarded out."[585]

A brave Irene found the situation at Glade tolerable because she taught alongside an Estonian woman who spoke the Doukhobors' first language, Russian. All the same, despite guards to prevent burnings and bombings, Irene was so afraid to leave the teacherage that she had someone else go to the post office for her to pick up and mail letters and parcels.[586]

Irene had good reason to be fearful. In the spring of 1932, during her second year at Glade, 600 British Columbia Doukhobor men and women were convicted of nudity, which the activist Sons of Freedom had adopted as a means of protest, and sentenced to three-year prison terms. Their children were initially put into orphanages and industrial schools in Vancouver and Victoria, but were then placed with other Doukhobor families on condition that they attend public school. Not surprisingly, shortly after Irene left Glade in the spring of 1933, after three years teaching there, and the school's protection was discontinued, it was torched. When almost completely rebuilt, the Glade school was again burned down.[587]

As the teacher she was, Irene did not give up on Doukhobor children. In the summer of 1933, she once again attended the Victoria normal school, this time taking courses in geography and singing. Irene did so preparatory to beginning a two-and-a-half-year stint, September 1933 to December 1935, in the small Doukhobor settlement of Kamanoe, across the Kootenay River from the larger Brilliant.[588] Once again she taught children whose first language was Russian and who, as explained in a school official's report for that time period, "supported by their parents, are defiantly absenting themselves from school."[589]

By the end of 1935, the pressure was too much. The ongoing tension of her work life and its confined circumstances caused Irene to take the 1936 calendar year off from teaching. Another factor was almost certainly her conviction that, however hard she worked in jobs few others would have accepted, she would always be perceived, first and foremost, as a "half-breed" and only subsequently as anything more. Not only did Irene lose faith in herself, on returning home she discovered that

Doukhobors long maintained the lifestyle they brought with them from Russia, first to Saskatchewan and then to British Columbia, here in Brilliant in about 1911. Royal BC Museum and Archives D-01929

the persons she most valued had now lost faith in her. She had always contributed to the family economy, causing her mother, Irene explained to me, to be displeased by her action. Only slowly did communication resume between mother and daughter.[590]

Irene returned to the classroom. In January 1937, in the middle of the next school year, she was sent to fill in at remote Baker Creek, fifty kilometres west of Quesnel, which she recalled as the "end of the world."[591] The next summer, intent on getting a better understanding of precisely why she had chosen to be a teacher, Irene took summer courses in Victoria in principles and techniques of teaching, educational measurement, and class organization and management.

Irene's commitment to Doukhobor children had not faltered, and 1937–38 she taught at Pass Creek, north of Castlegar. Adding to her teaching repertoire, the next summer she took courses in mental hygiene and measurement. Testifying to her capacity, in January 1939 she was transferred from Pass Creek to the larger Doukhobor community of

Otischenia as the school's principal.[592] When Irene was home at Easter, the school was bombed, which contributed to her decision that she had had enough adventure.[593]

If in the summer of 1939, on finally being offered a teaching position close to home, Irene left teaching Doukhobor children, the experience never left her. Irene reminisced at the time of her retirement about her decade with them: "Teaching there was a real challenge and provided a great deal of satisfaction. We had first to build a vocabulary for the children and then teach them to read."[594] In what was a compliment to teachers like Irene, a school inspector's report of the mid-1930s observed how, in the midst of many generalized criticisms about Doukhobor behaviour, "the children seem to be happy at school."[595]

Over half a century later, in February 1993, we drove at Irene's instigation to Agassiz, north of Chilliwack, to visit a hazelnut farm where she liked to buy nuts. Having made our purchases, we went at her suggestion along the Old Yale Road running north of the Fraser River. As we did so, she reminisced, almost as if it were yesterday, about coming back home along this route from teaching Doukhobor chldren and how each time she got to this point, she knew she would soon be home.[596]

That balmy winter day also revealed other aspects of Irene's character as a woman in-between all her life—as she considered herself to be. By this time, it was past three o'clock, and we had not had lunch. I suggested a couple of places we saw as we drove along and Irene demurred because they did not look safe. She asked me why people ate pizza and said she had never tried it because she was afraid that if she ordered it she might not like it and would be embarrassed to leave it with other people present. I saw the sign for Yarrow, settled by Mennonites, and half joked, given our previous conversation, that we could turn off. She said why not, since we were just wandering around, which in itself she considered a special, almost dangerous, pleasure. The town café was filled with men having afternoon coffee. We did so as well with Irene ordering a few drops of coffee with hot water. I suggested she also order a meal from the menu, but this was dangerous. She said she always has a lettuce and tomato sandwich, which was safe, and which she did. We chatted over our lunch and then returned to her Abbotsford condominium. As I left to return to Vancouver, she insisted that I take home half a cake that she got out of the freezer as a special treat and thank you, and it proved to be delicious indeed.

I think Irene had a good time that day. It was beautifully clear, and we kept seeing the mountains as we drove. Irene talked repeatedly about how they each had "names given by Indians," and how she wished she knew what the names were.[597] She was comfortable in herself.

FINALLY HOME AGAIN

It was only after almost two decades in the classroom that Irene was permitted to return home to teach. "I didn't get back here to this valley until 1939."[598] She reflected in an interview in the early 1980s on the reasons it took so long for her to return. "She had wanted to be near home, but she was well aware that local officials did not want a 'half-breed' teaching their children."[599] Irene had always been close to her parents. Emblematic of the relationship was her mother having over the years done all of Irene's "dressmaking—suits, coats, dresses, underwear," clothes that she considered to have been "real tailored."[600]

Yet, after being "at the homestead for a little while," the now forty-year-old Irene decided to live by herself. "When I came back here I felt that I wanted a home of my own so then I bought this lot and had the house built for myself."[601] Irene's doing so encouraged her self-confidence. Summing up one of our conversations,

Only in 1939, almost two decades after Irene began teaching and a decade before this picture was taken, was Irene offered a teaching position in the Fraser Valley, where she taught and served as school principal to her retirement in 1964. The Reach, Abbotsford, P11696

I jotted down how much "she came to enjoy her independence (having an income, being able to buy a house)."[602]

Reflecting the slowly changing times respecting persons of mixed Indigenous and white descent, it became possible for Irene to return to the Fraser Valley consequent on a job at North Poplar School in Abbotsford. It was offered to her in 1939 at a starting salary of $1,050—unchanged from her salary when she had begun teaching almost two decades earlier. She became school principal there before moving to Abbotsford Elementary School in 1960, where she remained until her retirement in June 1964. Irene continued to upgrade her credentials. In 1940 she took a crafts course and in 1941 and 1942 courses in woodwork and home nursing. During the 1950s, Irene took courses in Abbotsford on a variety of topics including automobile maintenance.[603]

Irene's retirement from teaching in the spring of 1964 finally gave her the freedom to do as she would, and to be whom she would be—but it would be short-lived. Within the year, Irene had moved her parents from their homestead into her home.[604]

> The winter of 64 was just terrible. It went down to zero, and everything froze tight at the homestead. The pipes froze and you couldn't put any fire in the cook stove because the pipes might break. So that meant my Dad would give up, and he gave up and said we would move out. That was a Saturday morning, that would be the 19th of December.... [A neighbour] brought a 1/2 ton truck up and we filled that truck with all we could, the clothes especially and the fruit and we came down and we got back to the house at 12 o'clock, and on the way down it was snowing, so we just got here in time. That was a terrible winter. I didn't get my car out again until about the 29th of January.[605]

In no way did Irene regret her changed circumstances. "I consider myself so lucky that my parents and I had these years together. My momma was a wonderfully patient woman, happy, cheerful and so good."[606] Julia Mathilda Kelleher died in 1967, Cornelius Kelleher two years later.

TIME FOR HERSELF

Following her father's death, Irene had time for herself and her own pleasures. "I felt I needed a change and I drove back up north," several times to visit Usk and Telkwa, where she had family and friends.[607] Irene also "travelled to the Holy Land and Europe, fulfilling a lifelong dream."[608]

In about 1985, Irene bought a large condominium in Abbotsford that she filled with the treasures of a lifetime, including portraits of her parents and other family members, a watercolour of her parents' long-time home, a number of large baskets made by her maternal grandmother, Ki-ka-twa or Julia, and the more contemporary Indigenous art

Irene's (second from the right) retirement from teaching gave the impetus to a social life that was still premised on service to others, as with her editing the history of the Ridgedale area of the Fraser Valley, where her parents had lived. She also came to value her Indigenous self as a fundamental part of who she was. ca. 1966. The Reach, Abbotsford, P14290

with which she increasingly identified. Irene's growing pride in her Indigenous inheritance comes through in a story she told me of some distant relatives inviting themselves over with the express purpose, they informed Irene, of having "come to collect Irene's Indian baskets," which they said she had promised them, to which Irene responded that she had done "no such thing" and they were going to a museum.[609]

Irene's self-confidence grew. Responding to a request from the Ridgedale Women's Institute "to write and record their local history," she took the lead respecting the community northeast of Abbotsford abutting the Fraser River where her family had long lived. "Much midnight oil was burned over that book, along with some joys and controversy, but mostly genuine praise."[610] *Wigwams to Windmills: A History of Ridgedale and Area* was published in 1977.[611] Irene's busy life included the monthly meetings of the Abbotsford District Teachers' Association, for which she was treasurer for thirteen years. She also served for several years as secretary of the Abbotsford Credit Union. Irene gave back in ample measure to the community.

HONOURING HER INDIGENOUS SELF

During these years Irene looked with growing pride at the totality of who she was. In the early 1980s, when she was in her early eighties, Irene took a course on British Columbia's Indigenous history at the nearby Fraser Valley College.[612] Frequently stopped and greeted on the street, often by former pupils, she reflected to me after one such encounter that she bet they were trying to figure out "what I am."[613] Another time, knowing I worked extensively at UBC with Indigenous students, she queried me: "Do I look Indian? How Indian do I look?"[614]

During one of our days together, at Irene's suggestion following our usual morning coffee, this day served with homemade baking powder biscuits, we visited Hatzic Rock. Located eighteen kilometres north of Abbotsford on the far side of the Fraser River, Hatzic Rock is now a National Historic Site. The large storied rock testifying to local Indigenous peoples' long history in the area was then a fairly recent find with which I was familiar from my position on the rock's provincial oversight body, BC Heritage Trust. Irene proudly told me how she had been a special guest at an Indigenous ceremony giving the rock "a burning and a bushing."[615]

Having paid our respects to the rock and its surroundings, Irene asked if I wanted to see the nearby cemetery where her parents were buried. There I noticed an adjacent identical family stone with a blank second line that Irene told me she had prebought for herself. We then drove some distance to the headstone of Irene's maternal grandfather, Joshua Wells, who was born in 1828 and died in 1898. Our next stop was Westminster Abbey, a seminary and community of Benedictine monks, one of whom she charmed into letting us visit the otherwise closed site.[616]

Irene increasingly shared her Indigenous heritage as a source of pride. The hurts she had passed over during her teaching days out of necessity she reworked as events that should and could have been remedied. Irene told me during one of our times together how Pat and Josephine Edwards' son Art fought during the First World War alongside Irene's "Uncle Andrew" Wells. During one of the battles, a member of the Edwards family later told Irene, Art was wounded and Andrew had gone to the front to rescue him despite the shelling. Hence Irene's heartfelt comment: "He should have been honoured, but he was a half-breed."[617]

Irene became more respectful of herself. At an Elders' lunch sponsored by the Stó:lō people at the Coqualeetza Educational Centre, which we attended together and where she received an award as the oldest Elder present, she proudly proclaimed, "I am one of you; I am a half-breed."[618] Perhaps Irene's finest moment came when she was honoured by North Poplar School, where she had taught so many years earlier, which named its library after her. Irene was finally accepted for who she was—a hard-working, multi-dimensional woman of mixed descent—and the hurt of a lifetime washed away.[619]

Irene died March 16, 2004, three months after her 103rd birthday.

POSTSCRIPT

It was within the context of Irene's growing pride in all the dimensions of her heritage that we encountered each other in the early 1990s at the suggestion of a mutual acquaintance. Irene had by then realized how much she was valued as a teacher and told me more than once of meeting a former student on the street, encounters I witnessed several times, who greeted her warmly and reminded her of the past they shared together. "If I had my life to live over, I don't think I could have planned it to work out better than it did. I was very happy as a teacher. I liked the children and had the feeling they liked me. I paid my own way in life."[620] Rare among women of her generation, white or Indigenous, Irene Kelleher displayed an independence of character, taking quiet pride in the freedom that came from making her own living.[621]

Irene built in her outlook and actions on two generations of Fraser Valley forebears. Her grandparents repeatedly crossed the boundaries between Indigenous and white at a time when the divisions were not yet so firmly set in place. Relationships between Indigenous people and white newcomers were initially more nuanced than many accounts would have them be.

Irene's parents nestled in intermediate spaces encompassing their extended families and like-minded friends. Mattie's skills as a seamstress encouraged conviviality even as it assumed deference on her part. Cornie's leadership during the Fraser River floods, in particular in 1948, appears to have had no racial dimension. "I don't know if he ever quit. I think he just went day and night."[622] In a commemorative book on the floods, this "Matsqui Farmer" was listed among those "pioneers... remembered by family and friends."[623] In similar fashion, as well as minding her own large family, Josephine Humphreys Edwards all her life cared for the health of those around her in times of need. Her reflection in her memoir is widely generalizable: "I did to the best of my ability make the best of what we had as so many of us had to do."[624]

In the third generation, Irene dared to venture out into the dominant white society. By so doing, she bore the brunt of pushing boundaries that were still to a considerable extent in place between Indigenous and white people. That Irene persisted as a teacher, and as a teacher of Doukhobor children in dangerous times, is remarkable.

For all of Irene's adventures, none of which she regretted in her conversations with me, her home and place of refuge was the Fraser Valley, as it had been for her parents and grandparents. To the extent that racism was long dominant across British Columbia and Canada, it was seemingly less so there, perhaps because so many of the first generation of white newcomers, arriving with the fur trade and in much larger numbers with the gold rush, had themselves pushed boundaries in their personal lives or at least had considered doing so.

Irene's story reminds us that our relationships with each other are more complex than we might have them be, or that we perceive them to be in the case of others. As in the Fraser Valley, surely then also elsewhere, people cared for each other in the everyday and in difficult circumstances. They helped when help was needed. Irene and her family and friends are in this sense just like you and me. Being half-and-half in the Fraser Valley, or for that matter elsewhere in British Columbia or Canada, was and is at the same time no easy matter.

Our meeting each other opened up the opportunity Irene sought to tell her story as she wanted it told, and so permit us all to reflect on her family's living between Indian—today more appropriately termed Indigenous—and white. We come to sense what it has meant to do so in the reality of the everyday.

Because I was teaching in the Faculty of Education at the University of British Columbia, Irene sensed a bond between us. Long after being a student there, she still strongly identified with UBC. Irene was consequently more confident than she might otherwise have been that I would respect her and her family for themselves rather than using their stories for my own purposes. She took very real pride in having been an early student at UBC, perhaps the earliest student of mixed Indigenous and white descent. During our years together, I tried to get Irene honoured by UBC, but it was perhaps too early in time for those in charge to be interested in persons caught between Indigenous and white, as opposed to being wholly Indigenous or wholly white, and my various overtures were rebuffed.

Irene considered I would respect her as a teacher, as indeed I did and do. Teaching is hard work, and to persist in doing it is commendable in any of us. Irene did so in circumstances where the opportunities that might otherwise have come her way were absent. Yet she continued and found niches, first in remote schools and then by reconfiguring herself as an early second-language teacher, taking on for almost a decade one of the most challenging jobs to be had in British Columbia, teaching Doukhobor children. It was only after almost two decades in the classroom that she was permitted to teach near home.

Irene's return to the Fraser Valley and her growing acceptance there for her qualities as a teacher and as a person were not only of her own doing, nor was it magnanimity on the part of school officials. The equation of skin tones with an inherent right on the part of the dominant society to discriminate at will was finally breaking down. Ever so slowly, the realization grew that racism was a set of behaviours based in fear, self-interest, and entitlement rather than in logical or reasonable argumentation. Individuals increasingly needed to prove themselves whatever their backgrounds rather than some backgrounds being dismissed out of hand and others tending to be accepted as a matter of course. As Irene firmly believed, "it's what you do with what you've been given that counts in this world."[625]

It was also the case, and still is all too often the case, as I noted to myself at the end of one of our conversations: "The general impression that comes through from this day is how tough Irene has had to be to survive—she knows exactly where she stands or rather may stand—she is always on guard and protecting herself against the slight that may come."[626] In one of our phone conversations, I asked Irene how to sum up her earlier years as a teacher most honestly, while she was being dispatched from pillar to post rather than being able to teach, as she wanted, near her home. Her response: "You can say I didn't get a school because I was a half-breed."[627]

Irene's story makes an important larger point, which is the capacity of human beings like herself, and her parents and grandparents before her, to persevere in extraordinary circumstances. It was not just them but also those around them who did so, none more so than Josephine Humphreys, whose white father had to choose between his political career and his daughter and sacrificed her to his ambition. The discrimination Irene and her family and their friends encountered, often when they least expected it, may have diminished over time, but it has in no way disappeared.

Irene's story also speaks to the mediating role of families. Whether we embrace, ignore, or deny our inheritance, we are each embedded in family. Irene's parents gave her the strength to be the best she could be as a teacher, and she in turn nurtured them when it was her time to do so. It was also the case, it might be argued, that Irene lived vicariously through her family instead of distinguishing herself as much as she could have as the discrete human being she was. Irene so respected her family that she seconded her life to their economic well-being. However we parse the possibilities, Irene's story is an object lesson in family dynamics.

Irene's story is about the everyday of all our lives, how we respond to others in our midst, and they to us. By coincidence, a descendant of Josephine Humphreys' beloved father later shared with me his father's story of finding himself alone in a pub in Lytton in the early 1950s. Introducing himself to an "Indian" sitting nearby as so-and-so "Humphreys, the Indian responded, 'Why, that's my name!'" It turned out they were both descended from the early provincial politician Thomas Humphreys, one from his "Indian family" in the language of the day whose two sons carrying his surname had made their lives as best they could at the edges of the edge; the other from Humphreys' white family, raised in privilege in Victoria and enjoying the fruits thereof.[628] While the two promised each other to keep in touch, they never did. In like manner, how fully and honestly we reveal ourselves to others, even if only in the moment, is at least to some extent ours to decide. Irene's story is in this sense all of our stories. Irene was caught up, from her perspective and also from that of much of the larger world around her, in the primacy long given to physical attributes, race by another name. Irene's sharing of her family's story gives each of us a pathway for our own lives. We all need to say at some point or the other, along with Irene, "I wouldn't let them put me down."[629] And, again to echo Irene, that "we got there in spite of them."[630]

ENDNOTES

Preface
1   University of the Fraser Valley, Civic Web, "President's Report."

Irene's Story
2   For guidance in taking on this role, I am indebted to Younging, *Elements of Indigenous Style.*

3   Conversation with Irene Kelleher, February 11, 1994.

4   References are not used in this paragraph so as not to single out individuals respecting common themes shared among a wide range of persons.

5   Oblate marriage and baptismal register, photocopy courtesy of Irene Kelleher.

6   Irene Kelleher, "Mother Kelleher's Family."

7   Cornelius Kelleher in "Early Pioneer Settlers."

8   "Kelleher Story," *Wigwams to Windmills*, 114.

9   See Barman, "Family Life at Fort Langley"; and Barman and Watson, *Leaving Paradise.*

10   Among such accounts are Robertson, Marcellus, and Dandy, *Mission's Living Memorials*; Sherwood, *Matsqui–Sumas–Abbotsford*; and Sleigh, *Mission as It Was,* whose "Early Community Builders" section comprises twelve white men and two white women. Cherrington's *The Fraser Valley* is more inclusive; *Matsqui, Sumas, Abbotsford Pioneer Stories* minimally so in that its 200 or so family stories include, if none of mixed white and Indigenous descent, four non-white families, one Sikh (319) and three Japanese families (151–52, 219–21, 281–83).

11   As examples, Schape, *Being Ts'elxwéyeqw*, passim; and Carlson, *Power*

of Place, 87–91 (Cooper, Commodore, Guiterraz, Lorenzeto). Neufeldt
and Siemens, *First Nations and First Settlers,* goes a different route
by considering the topic in separate sections of the book. While not
highlighting their mixed descent, Schape, *Being Ts'elxwéyeqw,* includes
numerous families historically to mixed descent.

12   Conversation with Irene Kelleher, November 20, 1992.
13   Pierson, *Making the White Man's West,* xvi, xxv.
14   Conversation with Irene Kelleher, December 2, 1992.
15   Conversation with Irene Kelleher, November 20, 1992.
16   Letter of Irene Kelleher to Jean Barman, April 5, 1993.
17   Barman, *The West beyond the West.*
18   Conversation with Irene Kelleher, February 11, 1994.
19   Conversation between Irene Kelleher and an unidentified third person,
     December 2, 1992; also letters to Jean Barman and to Roderick and
     Jean Barman.
20   Conversation with Irene Kelleher, November 20, 1992.
21   Conversation with Irene Kelleher, May 6, 1998. Not only are Imbert
     Orchard's interviews with the Kellehers available through BC Archives,
     one of them was given pride of place in Orchard's *Growing Up.*
22   Interview with Irene Kelleher by Crosby and Robertson.
23   Conversation with Irene Kelleher, December 2, 1992.
24   Conversation with Irene Kelleher, July 19, 1997.
25   Conversation with Irene Kelleher, May 6, 1998.
26   Conversation with Irene Kelleher, May 13, 1998.
27   For this information I am grateful to Irene's niece by marriage, Mar-
     lene Kelleher, telephone conversation, October 21, 2006.
28   Conversations with Irene Kelleher, December 2, 1992, and December
     11, 1996.

Irene's Paternal Inheritance

29   While Clark, "Saint Mary's Mission," provides useful information
     respecting the origins and operation of St. Mary's Mission, it identifies
     early pupils as solely Indigenous, as do numerous other histories of
     the institution.
30   Oblate marriage and baptismal register, photocopy courtesy of Irene
     Kelleher.
31   Irene Kelleher in "Memories," reprinted in *Wigwams to Windmills,* 118.

32 Interview with Cornelius Kelleher by Orchard. For an edited version of this interview, see Cornelius Kelleher, "Mission Boy," in Orchard, *Growing Up*, 21–39.

33 "Kelleher Story," *Wigwams to Windmills*, 114.

34 Interview with Cornelius Kelleher by Orchard.

35 Laing, *Colonial Farm Settlers*, 180.

36 Interview with Cornelius Kelleher by Orchard.

37 "Kelleher Story," *Wigwams to Windmills*, 112; and Irene Kelleher, "Irene Kelleher."

38 Irene Kelleher, "Job Family." Job's sister and her newcomer husband were the parents of Robert Johnson, who served as a magistrate at Sumas.

39 Beharrel, "Sketch."

40 Irene Kelleher, "Irene Kelleher."

41 Interview with Cornelius Kelleher by Orchard.

42 Laing, *Colonial Farm Settlers*, 107.

43 Interview with Cornelius Kelleher by Orchard.

44 Interview with Cornelius Kelleher by Orchard.

45 Interview with Irene Kelleher by Crosby and Robertson; and "Kelleher Story," *Wigwams to Windmills*, 112.

46 Beharrel, "Sketch"; for another version of the story, see "Teacher Retires after 41 Years," reprinted in *Wigwams to Windmills*, 117.

47 Conversation with Zoe Deroche Hewitt; also see the death registration of Deroche's son-in-law Antoine Danneau, 23421, BC, Vital Statistics, GR-2951.

48 *Fraser Valley Record,* March 23, 1922, and unidentified obituary, March 1922; in Mission Community Archives.

49 Sleigh, *Discovering Deroche*, 1.

50 Laing, *Colonial Farm Settlers*, 109; and interview with Cornelius Kelleher by Orchard.

51 Cornelius Kelleher in "Early Pioneer Settlers."

52 Watson, *Lives Lived,* 308.

53   BC, Vital Statistics, Marriage Registration, no. 41163.

54 Interview with Cornelius Kelleher by Orchard.

55 "Cornie Kelleher's Hunting Tales," unidentified clipping, 1957; and conversations with Irene Kelleher, June 25 and October 26, 1995, and March 28, 1998.

56   Conversations with Irene Kelleher, December 2, 1992, October 26, 1995, and March 28, 1998.

57   Conversation with Irene Kelleher, October 26, 1995.

58   Information copied from Oblate records, courtesy of Lyn Ross.

59   Interview with Irene Kelleher by Crosby and Robertson.

60   Laing, *Colonial Farm Settlers*, 107.

61   Laing, *Colonial Farm Settlers*, 105.

62   Canada, Department of Indian Affairs, *Annual Report*, 1874, pt. 2, 9; 1875, pt. 1, 48; 1877, 141, 171; 1879, 245; 1880, 220; 1881, pt. 2, 103; 1882, 252; 1883, pt. 2, 111; 1884, 121; 1885, 123. The grant for 1880–81 was for only nine months, probably due to a shortage of students.

63   Gresko, "Roman Catholic Missionary Effort," 57.

64   Sister Mary Theodore, "Sister Mary Lumena," 31, 32.

65   Canada, Department of Indian Affairs, *Annual Report*, 1882, 167.

66   I. Powell to Superintendent of Indian Affairs, March 3, 1885, in Canada, Department of Indian Affairs, RG 10, vol. 3694, file 14676, reel C-10121.

67   Cornelius Kelleher, "On Matsqui Indians."

68   Irene Kelleher, "Job Family"; and conversation with Irene Kelleher, September 17, 1993. Madeleine eventually married again, this time to George Whonnock, with whom she had Frank and Mary.

69   Interview with Irene Kelleher by Crosby and Robertson.

70   Beharrel, "Sketch."

71   "One of Earliest Pioneers."

72   Interview with Cornelius Kelleher by Orchard, and Edwards, "First Schoolmates."

73   Interview with Irene Kelleher by Robertson.

74   Interview with Irene Kelleher by Crosby and Robertson.

75   Canada, Census, 1881, 1877 NWN, household 305. The following pupils were named in the 1881 census as attending St. Mary's Mission school, along with their age and origin:

> Alonzo and Joseph Baker, born in about 1866 and 1869 of English origin
>
> George Barronowitch, born in about 1871 of English origin
>
> Philip Copp, born in about 1867 of English origin
>
> Colfax Cunningham, born in about 1869 of English origin
>
> John and Alphonse Dunn, born in about 1864 and 1880 of Irish origin

Cassie and Robert Gibson, born in about 1884 and 1869 of English
origin

William Hayward, born in about 1867 of English origin

John Hermes, born in about 1866 of English origin

Gustavus Herrling, born in about 1866 of English origin

Cornelius Kelleher, born in about 1872 with no given origin

Edward Mannion, born in about 1875 of no given origin

Sodain Michaud, born in about 1871 of French origin

Walter Peart, born in about 1873 of English origin

George and Henry Perry, born in about 1869 and 1872 of English
origin

Charles Reid, born in about 1866 of English origin

William Saunders, born in about 1870 of English origin

James and Joseph Taylor, born in about 1872 and 1866 of English
origin

Charles Woods, born in about 1871 of English origin

76 Waite, *Langley Story*, 36.

77 Laing, *Colonial Farm Settlers*, 100; Waite, *Langley Story*, 50; and Watson, *Lives Lived*, 228–29.

78 Waite, *Langley Story*, 249; Canada, Census, 1891, 2 NW, 14, #2, household 161; and Canada, Census, 1901, C8, New Westminster-Dewdney, Nicomen Municipality, household 16.

79 Interview with Cromar by Weir, 1972.

80 Edwards, handwritten memoir.

81 Interview with Cromar by Weir, 1972; interview with Jones; and marriage certificate of Patrick Edwards and Josephine Humphreys.

82 Jones, typescript, ca. 1935.

83 Weir, "Edwards Family"; interview with Cromar by Weir, 1972; and BC, Vital Statistics, Marriage Registration, nos. 41180, 41183, and 41195. A fourth possible child is Louis Edwards, who, at his marriage in 1880, described himself as born in Hope in about 1858, the son of Edwards and "Tsatsiemiate, Indian woman." BC, Vital Statistics, Marriage Registration, no. 41181.

84 BC, Vital Statistics, Marriage Registration, nos. 41180, 41183, and 41195.

85 Canada, Census, 1901, New Westminster, Dewdney, Mission, S Dist C, Mission municipality, households 30 and 31. Henry and Mary Edwards

gave their mother at the time of their marriages as "Siama, Indian woman," Patrick on his marriage as "Catherine Indian woman." BC, Vital Statistics, Marriage Registration, nos. 41180, 41183, and 41195.

86 Interview with Cromar by Weir, 1972.

87 Edwards in conversation with Mabel Nichols, recalled by Nichols in conversation with Jean Barman.

88 Hanson, "Strange Life-Story," *Vancouver Sun*, November 29, 1941; and Majors, "Northwest Discovery," *Journal of Natural History* 5, no. 22 (May 1984), cited in Coutts, *Cancelled with Pride*, 7.

89 Hanson, "Strange Life-Story," *Vancouver Sun*, November 29, 1941.

90 Hanson, "Strange Life-Story," *Vancouver Sun*, December 6, 1941.

91 Interview with Irene Kelleher by Crosby and Robertson.

92 Interview with Cornelius Kelleher by Orchard.

93 Irene Kelleher, "Irene Kelleher." The high quality of Cornelius Kelleher's writing and grammar is supported by C. Kelleher to C.T. Cooney.

94 Irene Kelleher, "Irene Kelleher"; and conversation with Irene Kelleher, November 20, 1992. Unfortunately, most of Cornelius Kelleher's diaries were destroyed in a house fire. Some sense of their contents survives in *Where All Trails Meet*, a writing project for which he gave access to his diaries.

95 Interview with Cornelius Kelleher by Orchard.

96 Interview with Cornelius Kelleher by Orchard.

97 Interview with Cornelius Kelleher by Orchard.

98 Interview with Cornelius Kelleher by Orchard.

99 Cornelius Kelleher in "Kelleher Story," *Wigwams to Windmills*, 112.

100 Interview with Cornelius Kelleher by Orchard.

101 "Kelleher Story," *Wigwams to Windmills*, 113.

102 Cornelius Kelleher in "Kelleher Story," *Wigwams to Windmills*, 113.

103 Interview with Cornelius Kelleher by Orchard.

104 "Kelleher Story," *Wigwams to Windmills*, 113.

105 Interview with Cornelius Kelleher by Orchard.

106 Interview with Irene Kelleher by Crosby and Robertson.

107 Interview with Cornelius Kelleher by Symons.

108 "Kelleher Story," *Wigwams to Windmills*, 112.

109 "Kelleher Story," *Wigwams to Windmills*, 112.

110 Interview with Cornelius Kelleher by Symons.

111 Interview with Cornelius Kelleher by Orchard.

112 "Kelleher Story," *Wigwams to Windmills*, 112.

113 Interview with Cornelius Kelleher by Symons.

114 Interview with Cornelius Kelleher by Orchard.

115 Interview with Cornelius Kelleher by Orchard.

116 "Kelleher Story," *Wigwams to Windmills*, 112.

117 "Kelleher Story," *Wigwams to Windmills*, 113.

118 Ravicz, Battung, and Buker, "Rainbow Women," 44.

119 Beharrel, "Sketch."

120 Interview with Cornelius Kelleher by Orchard.

121 Interview with Cornelius Kelleher by Orchard.

122 Beharrel, "Sketch."

123 Interview with Cornelius Kelleher by Orchard.

124 "Kelleher Story," *Wigwams to Windmills*, 113.

125 Interview with Cornelius Kelleher by Orchard.

126 "History of St. Mary's Mission."

127 Interview with Cornelius Kelleher by Orchard.

128 "Kelleher Story," *Wigwams to Windmills*, 113; and Pengilly, "Matsqui Man."

129 Cornelius Kelleher in "Kelleher Story," *Wigwams to Windmills*, 113.

130 Interview with Cornelius Kelleher by Orchard.

131 Beharrel, "Sketch."

132 Beharrel, "Sketch." According to land records, the approximately 45 acres that Kelleher acquired was part of a 150-acre pre-emption, recorded on June 26, 1862, by an Indigenous man named Joseph Swatelem, adjacent to Rev. d'Herbomez's claim and witnessed by Oblates George Blanchet and Charles Grandidier since the applicant was illiterate. It seems plausible that Swatelem, as well as another Indigenous man named Ironetselough, who pre-empted land next door, acted at the church's behest. Laing, *Colonial Farm Settlers*, 180.

133 Conversation with Irene Kelleher, December 2, 1992.

134 Irene Kelleher, "Irene Kelleher."

135 Interview with Irene Kelleher by Robertson.

136 "Kelleher Story," *Wigwams to Windmills*, 114; and Pengilly, "Matsqui Man."

137 "Kelleher Story," *Wigwams to Windmills*, 113–14.

138 Watt, *High Water*, 32.

139 "Kelleher Story," *Wigwams to Windmills*, 114.

140 "Kelleher Story," *Wigwams to Windmills*, 114.

141 Beharrel, "Sketch."

Irene's Maternal Inheritance

142 Interview with Irene Kelleher by Crosby and Robertson; and Irene Kelleher, "Julia M. Kelleher."

143 Beharrel, "Sketch."

144 Interview with Julia Mathilda Kelleher by Orchard.

145 Irene Kelleher, "Mother Kelleher's Family."

146 Interview with Julia Mathilda Kelleher by Orchard.

147 Cornelius Kelleher, "Things I Remember."

148 Interview with Irene Kelleher by Robertson; and Irene Kelleher, "Family Tree."

149 Beharrel, "Sketch."

150 Conversation with Irene Kelleher, December 2, 1992.

151 Interview with Irene Kelleher by Crosby and Robertson; Irene Kelleher, "Mother Kelleher's Family," "John Joshua Wells," "Mrs. Sarah Jane Lacroix," and "Chester Philip Wells."

152 Cornelius Kelleher, "Things I Remember."

153 Interview with Julia Mathilda Kelleher by Orchard.

154 Interview with Irene Kelleher by Crosby and Robertson.

155 Interview with Cornelius Kelleher by Orchard.

156 Laing, *Colonial Farm Settlers*, 107.

157 Watson, *Lives Lived*, 549.

158 Interview with Julia Mathilda Kelleher by Orchard; BC, Vital Statistics, Death Registration, no. 20706, BCA, GR-2951; and conversation with Irene Kelleher, December 2, 1992.

159 BC, Vital Statistics, Death Registration, nos. 20706 and 50891, and Marriage Registration, nos. 41190 and 41515.

160 Interview with Julia Mathilda Kelleher by Orchard.

161 Laing, *Colonial Farm Settlers*, 107.

162 Interview with Julia Mathilda Kelleher by Orchard.

163 Cornelius Kelleher in Wells, *Chilliwacks*, 188.

164 Interview with Julia Mathilda Kelleher by Orchard.

165 Interview with Julia Mathilda Kelleher by Orchard.

166 Interview with Irene Kelleher by Crosby and Robertson.

167 Ravicz, Battung, and Buker, "Rainbow Women," 44.

168 Interview with Cornelius Kelleher by Orchard.

169 Irene Kelleher, in "Memories," reprinted in *Wigwams to Windmills*, 119; Irene Kelleher, "Mother Kelleher's Family"; and BC, Vital Statistics, Death Registration, no. 4100.

170 Beharrel, "Sketch."

171 Irene Kelleher, "Memories of My Mother."

172 Conversation with Irene Kelleher, December 2, 1992.

173 Conversation with Irene Kelleher, March 28, 1998.

174 Conversation with Irene Kelleher, December 2, 1992.

175 Irene Kelleher, "Irene Kelleher."

176 Interview with Irene Kelleher by Crosby and Robertson.

177 Interview with Irene Kelleher by Crosby and Robertson.

178 Interview with Julia Mathilda Kelleher by Orchard; Irene Kelleher, "Mother Kelleher's Family"; and BC, Vital Statistics, Marriage Registration, no. 54-09-001227.

179 Conversation with Irene Kelleher, December 2, 1992.

180 Interview with Irene Kelleher by Crosby and Robertson.

181 Irene Kelleher, "Mrs. Sarah Jane Lacroix."

182 Conversation with Irene Kelleher, December 2, 1992.

183 BC, Vital Statistics, Pre-Confederation Marriage Records, 1859–1872, BC Archives, GR-3044.

184 Cornelius Kelleher, "Men Who Occupied Lands on Matsqui."

185 Irene Kelleher, "Memories of My Mother."

186 Interview with Julia Mathilda Kelleher by Orchard.

187 BC, Vital Statistics, Marriage Registration, no. 44249; and Canada, Census, 1901, Burrard, C11, Cassiar (Skeena), Hazelton and Interior, household 24.

188 Interview with Julia Mathilda Kelleher by Orchard.

189 Irene Kelleher, "John Joshua Wells."

190 Irene Kelleher, "Julia M. Kelleher."

191 Interview with Julia Mathilda Kelleher by Orchard.

192 Beharrel, "Sketch"; and Irene Kelleher, "Amos Louis Wells" and "Andrew Wells."

193 Conversations with Irene Kelleher, November 26, 1992, December 2, 1992, and April 25, 1993.

194 Conversation with Irene Kelleher, October 9, 1993.

195 Lists of British Columbia teachers in BC, Department of Education, *Annual Report,* 1883–89.

196 Edwards, "First Schoolmates"; and conversation with Irene Kelleher, December 2, 1992.

197 Interview with Julia Mathilda Kelleher by Orchard.

198 Interview with Julia Mathilda Kelleher by Orchard.

199 Irene Kelleher, "Julia M. Kelleher."

200 Interview with Julia Mathilda Kelleher by Orchard.

201 Canada, Census, 1881, 1877 NWN, household 305; and Edwards,
"First Schoolmates." Names below are a combined list with birth years
and origins taken from the 1881 census list. Not all of these students'
time at St. Mary's coincided with that of Mattie.

   Florence and Mary Baker, born in about 1874 and 1875 of English
     origin

   Josephine and Betsy Blanchard, born in about 1870 and 1871 of
     French origin

   Emily Mathilda and Clara Bradbury, born in about 1870 and 1875 of
     English or possibly Irish origin

   Ada, Letitia and Sarah Bulock/Bulevere, born in about 1869, 1871,
     and 1872 of English origin

   Ann and Lizzie Connier/Connor, Ann, born in about 1875 of French
     origin

   Fanny Cunningham, born in about 1866 of English origin

   Lizzie Dolens

   Josephine Dunn, born in about 1865 of Irish origin

   Mary Ellen Edwards

   Susan Everett, born in about 1867 of English origin

   Rosie, Mary, and Laura Fallerdo

   Caroline Laurence Florence

   Myria Flouss (?)

   Amelia, Katie, Mathilda, and Victoria Garypee

   Elvira Garner, born in about 1874

   Janet Gray, born in about 1874 of Scots origin

   Mathilda and Sophie Graff, born in about 1869 and 1873

   Eveline Grinder, born in about 1865 of German origin

   Mary Jane and Eddiss Hall

   Hellen and Laura Hayward

   Augustina Heffley

   Josephine Humphreys, born in about 1867 of English origin

   Josephine Hurling

   Mary Agnes and Mary Margaret Kamile/Kamul, Alefedss (?)

   Mary Theresa Kelleher

Helen [Ellen] and Mary Lacroix

Eugenie Louise Larochelle

Mary Kate Lorenzeto

Anastacia Matsqui

Anne Menefindo, born in about 1866 of no given origin

Mary Merryfield, born in about 1867 of English origin, also Annie
  Merrifield

Susan Miller, born in about 1874 of French origin

Mary Jane, Mary Catherine, and Agnes Paul, Thompson by descent

Catherine Percial, born in about 1869 of no given origin

Lydia and Lizzie Perkins

Theotiste, Elodie, and Melena Perrault, born in about 1869, 1872,
  and 1874

Susan and Maryanne Prest, born in about 1874 and 1870 of French
  origin

Catharine and Mary Ann Purcell, born in about 1869 and 1870

Adeline Semper/St Pierre, born in about 1866

Sarah Jane and Mathilda Wells

Mary Elizabeth Willing

Unrice and Edith Woods

202 Sister Mary Theodore, "St. Mary's Mission."

203 Canada, Census, 1881, NWN BEA 187, household 307.

204 Beaumont, "Charles Purcell Family"; "Pioneer's Death"; "A 'Fifty
  Eighter'"; BC, Vital Statistics, Marriage Registration, no. 41301; Canada,
  Census, 1891, 2 NW (Douglas), household 22; and Canada, Census,
  New Westminster C10-Dewdney (Harrison Lake/Douglas), household
  66.

205 "New Church"; Sleigh, *People*, 64–65; and Henry M. Keefer in Gomery,
  "Wedding."

206 St. Ann's Academy, "Register, 1865–1920"; and interview with Cromar
  by Weir, 1975.

207 Interview with Cromar by Weir, 1975.

208 Interview with Jones.

209 Edwards, handwritten memoir and chronology; and conversations
  with George, November 22 and 26, 1992.

210 See Halleran, "Humphreys," which disputes the East India Company
  claim; Humphreys' obituary in the *Times*, which queries it; and his
  obituary in the *Colonist*, which accepts it.

211 Edwards, handwritten chronology.

212 Hills, Diary, May 20, 1862 entry.

213 Edwards, handwritten memoir.

214 BC, Vital Statistics, Marriage Registration, no. 08-09-169496.

215 Edwards, handwritten memoir.

216 "Humphreys," *Times*; and "Humphreys," *Colonist*.

217 "Humphreys," *Times*.

218 Edwards in conversation with Nichols, recalled by Nichols in conversation with Jean Barman, November 22, 1992; and conversation with George, November 26, 1992.

219 Edwards, handwritten chronology.

220 Edwards, handwritten memoir.

221 Canada, Census, 1881, 188 Cariboo, sub-district Clinton Lillooet, households 41 and 45; 1891, Cariboo subdivision 2, sub-district 9 Clinton, household 22.

222 Edwards, handwritten memoir.

223 BC, Vital Statistics, Marriage Registration, no. 156; Humphreys, "Humphreys"; and Caroline Watkins Humphreys' pioneer form in BC Archives, Vertical Files, in which she gave her children's birthdates but also predated the marriage by a year. The actual date is unequivocally clear from BC, Vital Statistics, Marriage Registration, no. 156. For the birthdate of the first child, see also "Additional information supplied by Gwendolyn Humphreys Allen (Mrs. A.O. Allen) to Provincial Archivist, May 6, 1961, in BC Archives, Vertical Files. Thomas Stanley Humphrey's death certificate, with information given by his son Llewellyn, had him born on December 22, 1872, in Victoria, but his age as sixty-seven years, two months, and eight days, which would indicate 1873. See BC, Vital Statistics, Death Registration, no. 1940-1382.

224 Nesbitt, "Old Homes and Families."

225 "Humphreys," *Colonist*; "Humphreys," *Times*; and Halleran, "Humphreys."

226 Interview with Edwards by Symons; and conversation with George, November 26, 1992.

227 Conversation with Irene Kelleher, December 2, 1992.

228 "One of Earliest Pioneers."

229 Edwards, handwritten memoir.

230 Conversation with George, July 19, 1997.

231 Conversation with George, July 19, 1997.

232 Interview with Jones.

233 Edwards, handwritten chronology.

234 Conversation with George, November 26, 1992.

235 Irene Kelleher, "Mrs. Sarah Jane Lacroix."

236 Interview with Julia Mathilda Kelleher by Orchard.

237 Interview with Julia Mathilda Kelleher by Orchard.

238 Irene Kelleher, "James Darius Wells."

239 Beharrel, "Sketch."

240 Beharrel, "Sketch"; and interview with Julia Mathilda Kelleher by Orchard.

241 Interview with Julia Mathilda Kelleher by Orchard.

242 Beharrel, "Sketch."

243 Interview with Julia Mathilda Kelleher by Orchard.

244 Beharrel, "Sketch."

245 Interview with Julia Mathilda Kelleher by Orchard.

246 Interview with Julia Mathilda Kelleher by Orchard.

247 Interview with Julia Mathilda Kelleher by Orchard.

248 Interview with Julia Mathilda Kelleher by Orchard.

249 Interview with Julia Mathilda Kelleher by Orchard.

250 Conversation with Irene Kelleher, December 2, 1992.

251 Interview with Julia Mathilda Kelleher by Orchard.

252 Interview with Julia Mathilda Kelleher by Orchard.

253 Interview with Julia Mathilda Kelleher by Orchard.

254 Interview with Julia Mathilda Kelleher by Orchard.

255 Interview with Julia Mathilda Kelleher by Orchard.

256 Conversation with Irene Kelleher, December 2, 1992.

257 Interview with Julia Mathilda Kelleher by Orchard.

258 Canada, Census, 1891, 2 NW (14), household 77.

259 Conversation with Irene Kelleher, November 18, 1994.

260 Portrait in the possession of Irene Kelleher, who left her possessions and estate to her nephew.

261 Conversation with Irene Kelleher, May 13, 1998.

262 BC, Vital Statistics, Marriage Registration, no. 79-09-166203; and conversation with Irene Kelleher, April 25, 1993.

263 Interview with Julia Mathilda Kelleher by Orchard.

264 Notes on the Wells family in the Mission Community Archives.

265 Beharrel, "Pioneer's Recollections."

266 Mission Council, Minutes, August 4, 1894, in notes on Wells family in Mission Community Archives.

267 Court of revision, April 4, 1896, in notes on Wells family in the Mission Community Archives.

268 Beharrel, "Sketch."

269 Beharrel, "Early Settlers" and "Pioneer's Recollections"; and Riggins and Walker, *Heart of the Fraser Valley*, 208–9.

270 Edwards, handwritten memoir.

271 BC, Vital Statistics, Death Registration, no. 7922862; and interview with Irene Kelleher by Crosby and Robertson.

The Second Generation Joined Together

272 Sister Mary Lumena, "Diary 1868–1892."

273 Sister Mary Theodore, "St. Mary's Mission."

274 Bishop Louis-Joseph d'Herbomez, quoted in Gresko, "Roman Catholic Missionary Effort," 56.

275 Sister Mary Theodore, "St. Mary's Mission," summarizing Sister Mary Lumena, "Diary 1868–1892."

276 Sister Mary Theodore, "St. Mary's Mission."

277 BC, Vital Statistics, Marriage Registration, no. 41321.

278 *Forging*, 287.

279 Canada, Census, 1881, 1877 NWN, household 305.

280 BC, Vital Statistics, Marriage Registration, no. 41195; and Hanson, "Strange Life-Story," *Vancouver Sun*, December 6, 1941.

281 BC, Vital Statistics, Marriage Registration, no. 41180.

282 Census of Canada, 1901, New Westminster, Dewdney, Mission, S Dist C, Mission municipality, household 31; and interview with Cromar by Weir, 1972.

283 Conversation with Irene Kelleher, December 2, 1992.

284 BC, Vital Statistics, Marriage Registration, no. 41183.

285 Conversation with George, November 26, 1992.

286 Edwards, handwritten memoir.

287 "One of Earliest Pioneers"; and Edwards, handwritten memoir.

288 Conversation with George, November 26, 1992.

289 Conversation with George, November 26, 1992.

290 "One of Earliest Pioneers"; and interview with Cromar by Weir, 1975.

291 Edwards, handwritten memoir; and conversation with George, July 19, 1997.

292 Interview with Edwards by Symons.

293 Edwards, handwritten memoir.

294 Edwards, handwritten memoir, which documents her ongoing care of those in need around her.

295 Conversation with George, November 26, 1992.

296 Humphreys to daughter Josephine.

297 BC, Vital Statistics, Marriage Registration, no. 08-09-169496.

298 Humphreys to daughter Josephine.

299 Edwards, handwritten memoir.

300 Conversation with George, July 19, 1997; and Edwards, handwritten memoir.

301 Census of Canada, 1901, New Westminster, Dewdney, Mission, S Dist C, Mission municipality, household 31.

302 Edwards, handwritten memoir.

303 "One of Earliest Pioneers"; and "Hatzic Pioneer."

Irene's Parents

304 Conversation with Irene Kelleher, December 2, 1992.

305 "A 'Fifty Eighter'"; and "Pioneer's Death."

306 Edwards, "First Schoolmates."

307 Conversation with Irene Kelleher, December 2, 1992.

308 "A 'Fifty Eighter.'"

309 Gomery, "Wedding"; and BC, Vital Statistics, Marriage Registration, no. 98-09-11735. The wedding took place on April 19, 1898.

310 Gomery, "Wedding."

311 Sister Mary Theodore, "St. Ann's Convent."

312 Beharrel, "Sketch."

313 Beharrel, "Pioneer's Recollections."

314 Irene Kelleher, "Notes."

315 Irene Kelleher in "Kelleher Story," *Wigwams to Windmills*, 111.

316 "Kelleher Story," *Wigwams to Windmills*, 114.

317 Cornelius Kelleher, "Matsqui Dyke."

318 Beharrel, "Sketch."

319 Beharrel, "Sketch."

320 *Wigwams to Windmills*, 110, reprint of an undated clipping from the *Vancouver Sun* entitled "Survivor of 1894 Flood"; and Irene Kelleher in *Wigwams to Windmills*, 111.

321　Interview with Irene Kelleher by Crosby and Robertson; and Irene Kelleher in *Wigwams to Windmills*, 111.

322　Irene Kelleher in "Memories," reprinted in *Wigwams to Windmills*, 118.

323　Irene Kelleher, "Mother Kelleher's Family."

324　Conversation with Irene Kelleher, November 5, 1993.

325　Conversations with Irene Kelleher, November 20, 1992, and November 26, 1993.

326　Interview with Cornelius Kelleher by Orchard.

327　Irene Kelleher in *Wigwams to Windmills,* 111.

328　Interview with Irene Kelleher by Crosby and Robertson.

329　Interview with Cornelius Kelleher by Orchard.

330　Conversation with Irene Kelleher, December 2, 1992.

331　Ravicz, Battung, and Buker, "Rainbow Women," 45; and conversation with Irene Kelleher, April 25, 1993.

332　Conversation with Irene Kelleher, May 13, 1998.

333　Beharrel, "Sketch."

334　Irene Kelleher, "Irene Kelleher."

335　Irene Kelleher in "Memories," reprinted in *Wigwams to Windmills*, 118.

336　Conversation with Irene Kelleher, February 11, 1994.

337　Irene Kelleher, "Irene Kelleher."

338　"Kelleher Story," *Wigwams to Windmills*, 115.

339　"Irene Kelleher 1901–," 247.

340　Beharrel, "Sketch."

341　Interview with Irene Kelleher by Crosby and Robertson.

342　"Cornelius Kelleher," *Wigwams to Windmills*, 111.

343　Irene Kelleher, "Irene Kelleher."

344　"Cornelius Kelleher," *Wigwams to Windmills*, 111.

345　Irene Kelleher in "Memories," reprinted in *Wigwams to Windmills*, 118.

346　Conversation with Irene Kelleher, September 17, 1993.

347　C. Kelleher to Cooney.

348　"Kelleher Story," *Wigwams to Windmills*, 115.

349　Irene Kelleher in "Memories," reprinted in *Wigwams to Windmills*, 118.

350　Conversation with Irene Kelleher, November 20, 1992.

351 Irene Kelleher in "Memories," reprinted in *Wigwams to Windmills*, 119.

352 *Wigwams to Windmills*, 111.

353 "Cornelius Kelleher," *Wigwams to Windmills*, 112; and conversation with Irene Kelleher, November 20, 1992.

354 "Kelleher Story," *Wigwams to Windmills*, 115.

355 Conversation with Irene Kelleher, November 20, 1992.

356 Canute Anderson in Irene Kelleher, "Memories of My Mother."

357 Gerty Crist in Irene Kelleher, "Memories of My Mother."

358 Irene Kelleher, "Memories of My Mother."

359 Beharrel, "Sketch"; and conversation with Irene Kelleher, November 20, 1992.

360 Beharrel, "Early Settlers."

361 Beharrel, "Pioneer's Recollections."

362 Irene Kelleher, "Julia M. Kelleher."

363 Irene Kelleher in "Memories," reprinted in *Wigwams to Windmills*, 119; and conversation with Irene Kelleher, November 20, 1992.

364 Irene Kelleher, "Memories of My Mother."

365 "Receive Many Congratulations."

366 Irene Kelleher, "Memories of My Mother."

367 Irene Kelleher, "Julia M. Kelleher."

368 Irene Kelleher, "Memories of My Mother."

369 Edna Johnston in Irene Kelleher, "Memories of My Mother."

370 Conversation with Irene Kelleher, May 13, 1998.

371 Irene Kelleher, "Memories of My Mother."

372 Conversation with Irene Kelleher, November 5, 1993.

373 Irene Kelleher in *Wigwams to Windmills*, 111.

374 Conversation with Irene Kelleher, June 21, 1996.

375 Irene Kelleher, "Irene Kelleher."

376 *Wigwams to Windmills*, 22.

377 *Wigwams to Windmills*, 34.

378 Conversation with Irene Kelleher, February 11, 1994.

379 Conversation with Irene Kelleher, April 25, 1993.

380 Minerva Page in Irene Kelleher, "Memories of My Mother."

381 Conversations with Irene Kelleher, April 25, 1993, and May 13, 1998; and *Wigwams to Windmills*, 110.

382 Joseph Allard and Maxime Lavoie, whose offspring Narcisse Allard

and Justine Lavoie wed on October 9, 1864; see church records, St. Andrew's Catholic Church.

383 Canada, Census, 1881, district 191, Vancouver, Cowichan, household 69; and 1901, Vancouver, Cowichan, C2: North Cowichan, household 11.

384 Skinner, exercise book, in Skinner Papers, Manuscripts and Archives Division, New York Public Library, box 23; see also Barman, *Constance Lindsay Skinner*, 15.

385 A.E. (Ted) Johnston, "Pioneers of the Terrace Area."

386 "Kelleher Story," *Wigwams to Windmills*, 115; and conversation with Irene Kelleher, April 25, 1993. By another account, "C. Kelleher Was Elected Councilor by Acclamation," *Where All Trails Meet*, 38.

387 Beharrel, "Sketch."

388 Pengilly, "Matsqui Man."

389 "Kelleher Story," *Wigwams to Windmills*, 115.

390 Beharrel, "Early Settlers."

391 Conversation with Irene Kelleher, April 25, 1993.

392 Conversation with Irene Kelleher, November 20, 1992.

393 Interview with Cornelius Kelleher by Orchard.

394 "Cornelius Kelleher," *Wigwams to Windmills*, 17 and 110, a reprint of an undated clipping from the *Vancouver Sun* entitled "Survivor of 1894 Flood."

395 "Cornelius Kelleher," *Wigwams to Windmills*, 17; and in Watt, *High Water,* as Cornelius Kelleher, "Recollections of a Matsqui Old-Timer," 160.

396 *Wigwams to Windmills*, 110.

397 Irene Kelleher in *Wigwams to Windmills*, 111; also Gerry Adams in Watt, *High Water*, 180.

398 *Wigwams to Windmills,* 22.

399 Beharrel, "Pioneer's Recollections."

400 Irene Kelleher in *Wigwams to Windmills*, 111.

401 Cornelius Kelleher, July 1950, reprinted in *Wigwams to Windmills*, 112.

402 Irene Kelleher in *Wigwams to Windmills*, 111. On Sumas Lake's drainage, see Reimer, *Before We Lost the Lake*.

403 Conversation with Irene Kelleher, October 9, 1993.

404 Conversation with Irene Kelleher, October 30, 1998.

405 Conversation with Irene Kelleher, February 9, 1993.

406 Cade interviewed by Orchard, 1964; and unidentified obituary, March 1922, in Mission Community Archives.

407 Laing, *Colonial Farm Settlers*, 109; and Sleigh, *Discovering Deroche*, 9.

408 Canada, Census, 1891, 2 NW, 14, 2, household 161; Cade interviewed by Orchard, 1964; and BC, Vital Statistics, Marriage Registration, nos. 45893 and 06-09-052418.

409 "From Mrs. Faulkner's Scrapbook."

410 Hanson, "Strange Life-Story," *Vancouver Sun*, December 6, 1941.

411 Edwards, handwritten memoir.

412 Canada, Census, 1901, New Westminster, City, D4, household 40.

413 Frank Devlin, Indian Agent, to A.W. Vowell, Indian Superintendent, Victoria, December 4, 1897, Canada, Department of Indian Affairs, RG10, vol. 1451; Marriage Register, Queen's Avenue Methodist Church; and conversation with Ross, Abbotsford, October 9, 1993.

414 Garner, undated obituary; Canada, Census, 1881, NWN, household 357; Canada, Census, 1891, 2 NW, 14, #2, household 113; Canada, Census, 1901, New Westminster, A1, Chilliwack, Port Matsqui Municipality, household 36; and Melvin, *Post Office*, 55.

415 Hanson, "Strange Life-Story," *Vancouver Sun*, December 13, 20, and 27, 1941.

416 Conversation with Irene Kelleher, October 9, 1993; and Hanson, "Strange Life-Story," *Vancouver Sun*, December 13, 20, and 27, 1941.

417 Canada, Census, 1901, New Westminster, City, D4, household 40.

418 *The Progress*, June 24, 1908, reprinted as "River Boats Main Link to Coast."

419 Interview with George Jones.

420 BC, Vital Statistics, Marriage Registration, no. 41134.

421 Conversation with Irene Kelleher, November 20, 1992.

422 Conversation with Irene Kelleher, May 13, 1998.

423 Conversation with Irene Kelleher, November 20, 1992.

424 Interview with Irene Kelleher by Crosby and Robertson.

425 Conversation with George, November 26, 1992.

426 Gerard, *Gerard*, 9; and Gerard, *Converted*, 9, 14.

427 Gerard, *Converted*, 19, 25.

428 Gerard, *Gerard*, 25.

429 Gerard, *Gerard*, 27.

430 Gerard, *Gerard*, 26.

431 Gerard, *Gerard*, 26–27.

432 Gerard, *Gerard*, 25. On students' backgrounds, see Glavin, *Amongst God's Own*.

433 Gerard, *Gerard*, 25.

434 Gerard, *Gerard*, 26.

435 Gerard, *Gerard*, 25.

436 Conversation with Irene Kelleher, December 2, 1992.

437 BC, Vital Statistics, Death Registration, no. 2037.

438 Edwards, handwritten chronology.

439 For a retrospective perspective, see Halleran, "Humphreys."

440 Edwards, handwritten notes.

441 Irene Kelleher, "Julia M. Kelleher."

442 Irene Kelleher, "Memories of My Mother."

443 Irene Kelleher, "Julia M. Kelleher."

444 Irene Kelleher, "Memories of My Mother."

445 Beharrel, "Pioneer's Recollections."

446 Conversation with George, July 19, 1997.

447 Annie Faulkner in Irene Kelleher, "Memories of My Mother."

448 Conversation with George, July 19, 1997.

449 Conversations with Irene Kelleher, November 20, 1992, and April 25, 1993.

450 Conversation with Irene Kelleher, November 20, 1992.

451 Conversation with Irene Kelleher, November 20, 1992.

452 Conversation with Irene Kelleher, April 25, 1993.

453 Conversation with Irene Kelleher, November 20, 1992.

454 Canada, Census, 1891, 2NW, #9 Maple Ridge, household 125; and Miller, *Valley of the Stave*, 32.

455 Interview with Julia Mathilda Kelleher by Orchard; and BC, Vital Statistics, Marriage Registration, no. 41134.

456 Irene Kelleher, "Family Tree of Peter Douglas of Port Douglas" and "Mrs. Sarah Jane Lacroix."

457 Canada, Census, 1901, Burrard, C11, Cassiar (Skeena), Hazelton and interior, household 24.

458 BC, Vital Statistics, Death Registration, no. 50891.

459 "Pioneer Woman, Native of B.C., Buried Last Week"; Irene Kelleher, "Mrs. Sarah Jane Lacroix"; and BC, Vital Statistics, Death Registration, no. 49-09-002226.

460 Conversation with Irene Kelleher, November 18, 1994.

461 Irene Kelleher, "John Joshua Wells"; "John Joshua [underlining in original] Wells," 299–300; and interview with Irene Kelleher by Crosby and Robertson.

462 "John Joshua Wells."

463 Interview with Julia Mathilda Kelleher by Orchard.

464 Interview with Cromar by Weir, 1972.

465 Interview with Irene Kelleher by Crosby and Robertson.

466 Irene Kelleher, "John Joshua Wells."

467 Interview with Cromar by Weir, 1972.

468 Conversation with Irene Kelleher, November 18, 1994.

469 Irene Kelleher, "John Joshua Wells"; and BC, Vital Statistics, Death Registration, no. 2802.

470 BC, Vital Statistics, Death Registration, no. 23947; conversation with Irene Kelleher, November 18, 1994; and Irene Kelleher, "Chester Philip Wells."

471 Interview with Julia Mathilda Kelleher by Orchard.

472 Irene Kelleher, "James Darius Wells"; and Gent, "Doug Gent's History Pages."

473 Interview with Julia Mathilda Kelleher by Orchard.

474 Conversation with Irene Kelleher, December 2, 1992.

475 Conversation with Irene Kelleher, December 2, 1992.

476 Conversations with Irene Kelleher, November 20, 1992, April 25, 1993, November 18, 1994, and March 28, 1998.

477 Irene Kelleher, "James Darius Wells" and "Mother Kelleher's Family"; and BC, Vital Statistics, Death Registration, no. 15526.

478 Interview with Legace by Orchard.

479 Canada, Census, 1901, New Westminster, Dewdney, Mission, S Dist C, Mission municipality, household 31; and conversations with Irene Kelleher, December 2, 1992, November 26, 1993, and March 28, 1998.

480 Conversations with Irene Kelleher, December 2, 1992, and February 9, 1993.

481 Conversations with Irene Kelleher, December 2, 1992, April 25, 1993, and March 28, 1998.

482 Irene Kelleher, "Amos Louis Wells."

483 BC, Vital Statistics, Marriage Registration, no. 58148.

484 Conversation with Irene Kelleher, December 2, 1992.

485 "Coqualeetza Industrial School, Admissions and Discharges."

486 Conversation with Irene Kelleher, November 18, 1994.

487 Irene Kelleher, "Andrew Wells"; and conversation with Irene Kelleher, March 28, 1998.

488 "Coqualeetza Industrial School, Admissions and Discharges."

489 Irene Kelleher, "Andrew Wells"; and conversation with Irene Kelleher, April 25, 1993.

490 Irene Kelleher, "Andrew Wells"; and conversation with Irene Kelleher, March 28, 1998.

491 Irene Kelleher, "James Darius Wells"; and BC, Vital Statistics, Death Registration, no. 15526.

492 Irene Kelleher, "Andrew Wells"; BC, Vital Statistics, Death Registration, no. 54-09-001227; and conversation with Irene Kelleher, March 28, 1998.

493 Interviews with Cornelius Kelleher, September 11 and October 8, 1966, in Wells, *Chilliwacks*, 187, also back cover.

494 Conversation with Irene Kelleher, December 16, 1993.

495 Interview with Irene Kelleher by Crosby and Robertson.

496 Cornelius Kelleher, "On Matsqui Indians."

497 Interview with Cornelius Kelleher by Orchard.

498 Cornelius Kelleher in Wells, *Chilliwacks*, 190–91.

499 Interview with Cornelius Kelleher by Orchard; and conversation with Irene Kelleher, April 25, 1993.

500 Beharrel, "Sketch."

501 Interview with Irene Kelleher by Crosby and Robertson.

502 Conversations with Irene Kelleher, February 11, 1994, and March 28, 1998.

503 Ravicz, Battung, and Buker, "Rainbow Women," 45.

504 Interview with Cornelius Kelleher by Orchard.

505 "Kelleher Story," *Wigwams to Windmills*, 111–15.

506 BC, Vital Statistics, Death Registration, nos. 67-09-001732 and 69-09-015834.

507 Edwards, handwritten memoir.

508 Beharrel, "Pioneer's Recollections."

509 Irene Kelleher in "Memories," reprinted in *Wigwams to Windmills*, 119.

510 Irene Kelleher and Cornelius Kelleher, "Kelleher Farm."

511 "Kelleher Story," *Wigwams to Windmills*, 115.

512 Conversations with Irene Kelleher, May 6 and 13, 1998.

513 Interview with Irene Kelleher by Crosby and Robertson.

514 Irene Kelleher in *Wigwams to Windmills*, 111.

515 Beharrel, "Sketch."

516 *Wigwams to Windmills*, 34, 111, 119; interview with Irene Kelleher by Crosby and Robertson; and BC, Vital Statistics, Death Registration, nos. 67-09-001732 and 69-09-015834.

Irene Alone

517 Irene Kelleher in "Memories," reprinted in *Wigwams to Windmills*, 118.

518 "Kelleher Story," *Wigwams to Windmills*, 117.

519 Irene Kelleher, "Mother Kelleher's Family."

520 Irene Kelleher in "Memories," reprinted in *Wigwams to Windmills*, 118.

521 Irene Kelleher, "Irene Kelleher."

522 Conversations with Irene Kelleher, November 20, 1992, and April 25, 1993.

523 Irene Kelleher in "Memories," reprinted in *Wigwams to Windmills*, 118–19.

524 Irene Kelleher, "Irene Kelleher."

525 Irene Kelleher in "Memories," reprinted in *Wigwams to Windmills*, 119; and conversation with Irene Kelleher, April 25, 1993.

526 Conversation with Irene Kelleher, September 17, 1993.

527 Conversation with Irene Kelleher, April 25, 1993.

528 Conversation with Irene Kelleher, February 11, 1994.

529 From a copy of a yearbook in Irene's possession that she showed me.

530 Irene Kelleher in "Memories," reprinted in *Wigwams to Windmills*, 119.

531 Irene Kelleher in "Memories," reprinted in *Wigwams to Windmills*, 119.

532 Conversation with Irene Kelleher, April 25, 1993.

533 Conversation with Irene Kelleher, February 11, 1994.

534 Conversation with Irene Kelleher, April 25, 1993.

535 Interview with Irene Kelleher by Crosby and Robertson.

536 Beharrel, "Sketch"; and conversation with Irene Kelleher, April 25, 1993.

537 Conversation with Irene Kelleher, April 25, 1993.

538 Conversations with Irene Kelleher, April 25, 1993, and March 28, 1998.

539 Conversation with Irene Kelleher, November 18, 1994.

540 Irene Kelleher's teaching dates are courtesy of Irene Kelleher, as confirmed in the annual "List of British Columbia Teachers in British Columbia" in BC, Department of Education, *Annual Reports*. Information on the Usk School comes from Whitlow, "Usk," in Gent, "Doug Gent's History Pages."

541 Information on individual teachers and schools comes from BC, Department of Education, *Annual Reports*.

542 Irene Kelleher in "Memories," reprinted in *Wigwams to Windmills*, 119.

543 Irene Kelleher in "Memories," reprinted in *Wigwams to Windmills*, 119.

544 Conversations with Irene Kelleher, March 18 and May 13, 1998.

545 Conversation with Irene Kelleher and her photograph album she shared with me, April 25, 1993.

546 Irene Kelleher in "Memories," reprinted in *Wigwams to Windmills*, 119.

547 Conversation with Irene Kelleher, April 25, 1993.

548 Conversations with Irene Kelleher, November 20, 1992, and April 25, 1993.

549 Conversation with Irene Kelleher, April 25, 1993.

550 Conversation with Irene Kelleher, November 20, 1992.

551 Conversation with Irene Kelleher, April 25, 1993.

552 Conversation with Irene Kelleher, November 20, 1992.

553 Conversations with Irene Kelleher, November 20, 1992, and April 25, 1993.

554 Conversation with Irene Kelleher, August 5, 1994.

555 Conversation with Irene Kelleher by Mabel Pennier, courtesy of Mabel Pennier, November 10, 1992.

556 Conversation with Irene Kelleher, May 13, 1998.

557 Conversation with Irene Kelleher, August 5, 1994.

558 Conversation with Irene Kelleher, February 11, 1994.

559 Conversation with Irene Kelleher, December 11, 1996.

560 Conversation with Irene Kelleher, July 19, 1997.

561 Irene Kelleher in "Memories," reprinted in *Wigwams to Windmills*, 119.

562 Irene Kelleher, "Irene Kelleher"; and conversation with Irene Kelleher, May 13, 1998.

563 Conversation with Irene Kelleher, December 2, 1992.

564 Conversation with Irene Kelleher, April 25, 1993.

565 Irene Kelleher, "Irene Kelleher."

566 Conversation with Irene Kelleher, November 20, 1992.

567 Conversations with Irene Kelleher, November 20, 1992, and May 13, 1998.

568 *Forging*, 400.

569 Irene Kelleher, "Irene Kelleher."

570 Conversation with Irene Kelleher, February 11, 1994; and Bolton and Daly, *Xwelíqwiya: The Life of a Stó:lō Matriarch*, 38.

571 Beharrel, "Sketch."

572 Irene Kelleher in "Memories," reprinted in *Wigwams to Windmills*, 119.

573 Conversation with Irene Kelleher, November 20, 1992.

574 This section draws for its general information on Ashworth, *Forces*, 133–72; Janzen, *Limits*, 128–35; and Tarasoff, *Plakun Trava*, supplemented by Woodcock and Avakumovic, *Doukhobors*, and Hawthorn's edited *Doukhobors of British Columbia*.

575 Conversations with Irene Kelleher, November 20 and December 2, 1992.

576 Orchard, *Floodland*, 40.

577 Goodfellow, *Memories of Pioneer Life*, 16, 39–40.

578 Conversations with Irene Kelleher, December 2, 1992, and February 9, 1993; Riggins and Walker, *Heart of the Fraser Valley*, 236; "Philip Hudson Sheffield"; and BC, Vital Statistics, Marriage Registration, no. 79-09-1662031.

579 Julia and Cornelius Kelleher in Wells, *Chilliwacks*, 188.

580 Conversation with Irene Kelleher, October 30, 1998; and Irene Kelleher, "Irene Kelleher."

581 Conversation with Irene Kelleher, May 13, 1998.

582 Statement by Brilliant Doukhobors, 1912, in Tarasoff, *Plakun Trava*, 118–19.

583 Nesteroff, "Ferry Tale Existence." Doukhobor settlements in British Columbia are listed in Tarasoff, *Plakun Trava*, 250, with a map of the principal sites on 105.

584 Interview with Irene Kelleher by Crosby and Robertson; and "Teacher Retires after 41 Years," reprinted in *Wigwams to Windmills*, 117.

585 Irene Kelleher in "Memories," reprinted in *Wigwams to Windmills*, 119.

586 Conversation with Irene Kelleher, April 25, 1993.

587 Nesteroff, "Ferry Tale Existence."

588 Irene Kelleher, "Irene Kelleher."

589 F.A. Jewett in school inspector's report for 1935–36, quoted in Ashworth, *Forces*, 154.

590 Conversation with Irene Kelleher, October 30, 1998.

591 "Teacher Retires after 41 Years," reprinted in *Wigwams to Windmills*, 117.

592 Irene Kelleher, "Irene Kelleher"; and conversation with Irene Kelleher, November 18, 1994.

593 Beharrel, "Sketch."

594 "Teacher Retires after 41 Years," reprinted in *Wigwams to Windmills*, 117.

595 School inspector's report, 1935–36, quoted in Ashworth, *Forces,* 154.

596 Conversation with Irene Kelleher, February 9, 1993.

597 Conversation with Irene Kelleher, February 9, 1993.

598 Interview with Irene Kelleher by Crosby and Robertson.

599 Ravicz, Battung, and Buker, "Rainbow Women," 44–45.

600 Irene Kelleher, "Memories of My Mother" and "Irene Kelleher."

601 Interview with Irene Kelleher by Crosby and Robertson.

602 Conversation with Irene Kelleher, November 20, 1992.

603 Irene Kelleher, "Irene Kelleher."

604 Irene Kelleher in "Memories," reprinted in *Wigwams to Windmills*, 119.

605 Interview with Irene Kelleher by Crosby and Robertson.

606 Irene Kelleher in "Memories," reprinted in *Wigwams to Windmills*, 119.

607 "Teacher Retires after 41 Years," reprinted in *Wigwams to Windmills*, 117.

608 Ravicz, Battung, and Buker, "Rainbow Women," 45; and Irene Kelleher in "Memories," reprinted in *Wigwams to Windmills*, 119.

609 Conversation with Irene Kelleher, April 25, 1993.

610 Irene Kelleher, "Irene Kelleher."

611 Irene Kelleher, "Irene Kelleher"; and *Wigwams to Windmills.*

612 Ravicz, Battung, and Buker, "Rainbow Women," 45.

613 Conversation with Irene Kelleher, February 9, 1993.

614 Conversation with Irene Kelleher, March 17, 1995.

615 Conversation with Irene Kelleher, February 9, 1993.

616 Conversation with Irene Kelleher, February 9, 1993.

617 Conversation with Irene Kelleher, April 25, 1993.

618 Irene Kelleher at Coqualeetza Elders' Christmas lunch, December 11, 1996.

619 Conversation with Irene Kelleher, March 28, 1998.

620 Irene Kelleher in "Memories," reprinted in *Wigwams to Windmills*, 119.

621 Conversation with Irene Kelleher, November 20, 1992.

622 Dave Faulkner, "Sandbags and Boils," in Watt, *High Water*, 180.

623 "In Recognition" in Watt, *High Water*, 305.

624 Edwards, handwritten memoir.

625 Irene Kelleher, cited in Ravicz, Battung, and Buker, "Rainbow Women," 45.

626 Conversation with Irene Kelleher, December 2, 1992.

627 Conversation with Irene Kelleher, August 2, 1998.

628 Ronald Humphreys and Jean Foote Humphreys, email exchange, March 10, 2000.

629 Conversation with Irene Kelleher, November 20, 1992.

630 Conversation with Irene Kelleher, December 2, 1992.

SOURCES CITED

Allen, Gwendolyn Humphreys (Mrs. A.O. Allen). British Columbia [BC] Archives, Vertical Files.

Ashworth, Mary. *The Forces Which Shaped Them: A History of the Education of Minority Group Children in British Columbia*. Vancouver: New Star Books, 1979.

Barman, Jean. *Constance Lindsay Skinner: Writing on the Frontier*. Toronto: University of Toronto Press, 2002.

Barman, Jean. "Family Life at Fort Langley," British Columbia Historical News 32, no. 4 (Fall 1999): 16–23.

Barman, Jean. *The West beyond the West: A History of British Columbia*. 3rd ed. Toronto: University of Toronto Press, 2007.

Barman, Jean, and Bruce Watson. *Leaving Paradise: Indigenous Hawaiians in the Pacific Northwest, 1787–1898.* Honolulu: University of Hawai'i Press, 2006.

Beaumont, Donna. "Charles Purcell Family." Typescript courtesy of Donna Beaumont.

Beharrel, Mrs. L.T. [Page]. "Pioneer's Recollections of Well Known Resident." Unidentified clipping, 1963, in Mission Community Archives.

Beharrel, Rosell [Page]. "A Sketch of the Life of Mr. and Mrs. Cornelius Kelleher as Told to Rosell [Page] Beharrel in March, 1957." Typescript courtesy of Irene Kelleher.

Beharrel, Mrs. [Rosell Page]. "Early Settlers Remember Her Many Kindnesses." *Abbotsford, Sumas and Matsqui News*, April 10, 1963.

Bolton, Rena Point, and Richard Daly. *Xwelíqwiya: The Life of a Stó:lō Matriarch*. Edmonton: AU Press, 2013.

British Columbia, Department of Education. *Annual Reports.*

British Columbia, Division of Vital Statistics. Death Registrations. BC Archives, GR-2951.

British Columbia, Division of Vital Statistics. Marriage Registrations. BC Archives, GR-2962.

British Columbia, Division of Vital Statistics. Pre-Confederation Marriage Records, 1859–1872. BC Archives, GR-3044.

Cade, Mrs. O.M. [Olivia]. Interview by Imbert Orchard, June 1, 1964. BC Archives, tape 761.

Canada. Census, 1881, 1891, 1901. Library and Archives Canada.

Canada, Department of Indian Affairs. *Annual Reports.*

Canada, Department of Indian Affairs. Library and Archives Canada, RG10.

Carlson, Keith Thor. *The Power of Place, the Problem of Time: Aboriginal Identity and Historical Consciousness in the Cauldron of Colonialism.* Toronto: University of Toronto Press, 2010.

Cherrington, John A. *The Fraser Valley: A History*. Madeira Park, BC: Harbour Publishing, 1992.

Clark, Melanie Ann Jones. "Saint Mary's Mission (Mission City, British Columbia) 1861 to 1900." Master's thesis, Department of Geography, University of British Columbia, 1993.

"Coqualeetza Industrial School, Admissions and Discharges." United Church Archives, Vancouver School of Theology.

"Corney Kelleher's Hunting Tales: Fish, Deer and Ducks at Hatzic." Unidentified clipping, 1957. Mission Community Archives.

Coutts, Cecil C. *Cancelled with Pride: A History of Chilliwack Area Post Offices 1865–1993.* Privately printed, 1993.

Cromar, Virginia Edwards. Interview by Betty Weir. September 4, 1972. BC Archives, tape 71.

Cromar, Virginia Edwards. Interview by Betty Weir. April 8, 1975, under an LIP grant. Mission Community Archives.

"Early Pioneer Settlers Led Busy, Colorful Lives." *Fraser Valley Record*, January 8, 1958.

Edwards, Josephine Humphreys. "First Schoolmates 1874 St. Mary's." Handwritten notes. Courtesy of Rosemarie George.

Edwards, Josephine Humphreys. Handwritten chronology. Courtesy of Rosemarie George.

Edwards, Josephine Humphreys. Handwritten memoir [1953]. Courtesy of Rosemarie George.

Edwards, Josephine Humphreys. Handwritten notes. Courtesy of Rosemarie George.

Edwards, Josephine Humphreys. Interview by Guy Symons, ca. 1953.

Edwards, Patrick, and Josephine Humphreys. Marriage certificate, St. Mary's Mission, June 26, 1884. Courtesy of Rosemarie George.

"A 'Fifty Eighter [George Goodwin Purcell].'" *Colonist*, March 11, 1902. Courtesy of Rosemarie George.

Forging a New Hope: Struggles and Dreams, 1848–1948. Hope: Hope and District Historical Society, 1984.

Fraser Valley Record. March 23, 1922.

"From Mrs. Faulkner's Scrapbook." Typescript in Mission Community Archives.

Garner, Robert. Undated obituary. BC Archives, Vertical Files.

Gent, Doug. "Doug Gent's History Pages." Online at www.gent-family.com. Accessed December 20, 2018.

George, Rosemarie Harper. Conversations with Jean Barman, November 22 and 26, 1992, November 26, 1993, and July 19, 1997.

Gerard, Bernice. *Bernice Gerard: Today and for Life*. Burlington, ON: Welch Publishing Co., 1988.

Gerard, Bernice. *Converted in the Country: The Life Story of Bernice Gerard as Told by Herself*. Jacksonville, FL: McColl-Gerard Publications, 1956.

Glavin, Terry, and former students of St. Mary's. *Amongst God's Own: The Enduring Legacy of St. Mary's Mission*. Mission, BC: St. Mary's Indian Friendship Centre Society, 2002.

Gomery, Percy. "Wedding at Old Fort Douglas." *Province*, November 15, 1941.

Goodfellow, Florence. *Memories of Pioneer Life in British Columbia: A Short History of the Agassiz Family*. Hope, BC: Harrison Lake Historical Society, 1982.

Gresko [Kennedy], Jacqueline Judith. "Roman Catholic Missionary Effort and Indian Acculturation in the Fraser Valley 1860–1900." Unpublished BC honour's essay, Department of History, University of British Columbia, 1969.

Halleran, Michael F.H. "Thomas Basil Humphreys." *Dictionary of Canadian Biography*. Online.

Hanson, Edna Brandon. "The Strange Life-Story of Captain Charlie Gardner [based on interviews with him]." *Vancouver Sun*, November 29 and December 6, 13, 20, and 27, 1941, magazine section.

"Hatzic Pioneer." October 15, 1958. Mission Community Archives.

Hawthorn, Harry B., ed. *The Doukhobors of British Columbia*. Vancouver: University of British Columbia and J.M. Dent & Sons, 1955.

Hewitt, Zoe Deroche. Conversation with unknown person. BC Archives, Vertical Files.

Hills, Bishop George. Diary. Anglican Church, Ecclesiastical Province of British Columbia, Archives.

"History of St. Mary's Mission: One of Struggle, Courage, Faith." *Fraser Valley Record*, October 25, 1950.

"Hon. Thomas Basil Humphreys." *Colonist*, August 27, 1890.

"Hon. Thomas B. Humphreys." *Times*, August 26, 1890.

Humphreys, Caroline Watkins. Pioneer form. BC Archives, Vertical Files.

Humphreys, Jean Foote. "The Honourable Thomas Basil Humphreys: A Controversial Contributor to Change in Early BC Politics." *BC Historical News* 35, no. 3 (Summer 2001): 9–15.

Humphreys, Ronald, and Jean Foote. Email exchange, March 10, 2000.

Humphreys, T.B., to daughter Josephine, Victoria, January 4, 1885. Letter courtesy of Rosemarie George.

"Irene Kelleher 1901–." In Daphne Sleigh, ed. *One Foot on the Border: A History of Sumas Prairie & Area* (Sumas Prairie, BC: Sumas Prairie and Area Historical Society), 247–48.

Janzen, William. *Limits on Liberty: The Experience of Mennonite, Hutterite, and Doukhobor Communities in Canada*. Toronto: University of Toronto Press, 1990.

"John Joshua Wells." *Abbotsford, Sumas and Matsqui News*, April 5, 1947.

"John Joshua [underlining in original] Wells 1865/68–1947." In Daphne Sleigh, ed. *One Foot Across the Border: A History of Sumas Prairie & Area* (Sumas Prairie, BC: Sumas Prairie and Area Historical Society), 299–300.

Johnston, A.E. (Ted). "Pioneers of the Terrace Area." Terrace: Heritage Park Museum, 1989. Typescript in Heritage Park Museum, Terrace.

Jones, George. Interview by unknown person, Mission, January 12, 1979. Mission Community Archives.

Jones, Harry. Typescript, ca. 1935. British Columbia Archives, Add. Ms. 361, file 1.

Kelleher, Cornelius. "Cornelius Kelleher, July 1950." Reprinted in *Wigwams to Windmills: A History of Ridgedale and Area*. Abbotsford, BC: Ridgedale Women's Institute, 1977, 111.

Kelleher, Cornelius. Interview by Guy Symons. Mission Community Archives, no. 1689.

Kelleher, Cornelius. Interview by Imbert Orchard, March 1963. British Columbia Archives, tape 705.

Kelleher, Cornelius. "The Matsqui Dyke." Typescript courtesy of Irene Kelleher.

Kelleher, Cornelius. "Men Who Occupied Lands on Matsqui." Notes courtesy of Irene Kelleher.

Kelleher, Cornelius. "On Matsqui Indians." Notes courtesy of Irene Kelleher.

Kelleher, Cornelius. "Things I Remember." Typescript in Mission Community Archives.

Kelleher, C., to C.T. Cooney, Mission City, January 25, 1910. C.T. Cooney File, Kamloops Archives, 69.5.2.

Kelleher, Irene. "Amos Louis Wells." Typescript courtesy of Irene Kelleher.

Kelleher, Irene. "Andrew Wells." Typescript courtesy of Irene Kelleher.

Kelleher, Irene. "Chester Philip Wells." Typescript courtesy of Irene Kelleher.

Kelleher, Irene. Conversations with Jean Barman, Abbotsford, British Columbia, November 20, 1992; December 2, 1992; February 9, 1993; April 25, 1993; September 17, 1993; October 9, 1993; November 5, 1993; November 26, 1993; December 16, 1993; February 11, 1994; August 5, 1994; November 18, 1994; March 17, 1995; June 25, 1995; October 26, 1995; December 13, 1995; June 21, 1996; December 11, 1996; July 19, 1997; March 28, 1998; May 6, 1998; May 13, 1998; August 2, 1998; October 30, 1998; March 10, 1999.

Kelleher, Irene. "Family Tree of Peter Douglas of Port Douglas." Notes courtesy of Irene Kelleher.

Kelleher, Irene. Interview by D. Crosby and M. Robertson under LIP grant, February 27, 1975. Courtesy of Irene Kelleher.

Kelleher, Irene. Interview by M. Robertson under LIP project, February 24, 1975. Transcript courtesy of Irene Kelleher.

Kelleher, Irene. "Irene Kelleher." Autobiographical typescript courtesy of Irene Kelleher.

Kelleher, Irene. "James Darius Wells." Typescript courtesy of Irene Kelleher.

Kelleher, Irene. "The Job Family of Nooksack." Notes courtesy of Irene Kelleher.

Kelleher, Irene. "John Joshua Wells." Typescript courtesy of Irene Kelleher.

Kelleher, Irene. "Julia M. Kelleher." Notes courtesy of Irene Kelleher.

Kelleher, Irene. Letters to Jean Barman, April 5, 1993, and to Roderick and Jean Barman, May 4, 1993.

Kelleher, Irene, in "Memories Are Made of This." *Fraser Valley Magazine*,

August 23, 1976. Reprinted in *Wigwams to Windmills: A History of Ridgedale and Area*. Abbotsford, BC: Ridgedale Women's Institute, 1977, 119.

Kelleher, Irene. "Memories of My Mother—Julia Mathilda Kelleher." Notes courtesy of Irene Kelleher.

Kelleher, Irene. "Mother Kelleher's Family." Notes courtesy of Irene Kelleher.

Kelleher, Irene. "Mrs. Sarah Jane Lacroix." Typescript courtesy of Irene Kelleher.

Kelleher, Irene. "Notes." Typescript courtesy of Irene Kelleher.

Kelleher, Irene, and Cornelius Kelleher. "The Kelleher Farm." Notes courtesy of Irene Kelleher.

Kelleher, Julia Mathilda. Interview by Imbert Orchard, March 1963. BC Archives, tape 704.

Kelleher, Marlene. Telephone conversation, October 21, 2006.

"Kelleher Story Link with Pioneer Days." *Abbotsford, Sumas and Matsqui News*, July 12 and 19, 1950. Reprinted in *Wigwams to Windmills: A History of Ridgedale and Area*. Abbotsford, BC: Ridgedale Women's Institute, 1977, 114.

Laing, F.W. *Colonial Farm Settlers on the Mainland of British Columbia, 1858–1871*. Victoria, 1939. Typescript in University of British Columbia Library, Special Collections.

Legace, Peter. Interview by Imbert Orchard. BC Archives, tape 760.

Mary Lumena, Sister. "Diary 1868–1892," 2nd copy by a sister copyist, p. 45, in Archives, Sisters of St. Ann, Victoria, relocated to Provincial Archives of British Columbia.

Mary Theodore, Sister. "St. Ann's Convent, New Westminster, B.C., 1865." Typescript in Archives, Sisters of St. Ann, Victoria, relocated to Provincial Archives of British Columbia.

Mary Theodore, Sister. "St. Mary's Mission Matsqui" [1943]. Typescript in Archives, Sisters of St. Ann, Victoria, relocated to Provincial Archives of British Columbia.

Mary Theodore, Sister. "Sister Mary Lumena #42." Typescript in Sisters of St. Ann, Victoria, Archives, RG 1, S.24, relocated to Provincial Archives of British Columbia.

Matsqui, Sumas, Abbotsford Pioneer Stories, 1890–1950. Abbotsford BC: MSA Museum Society, 2013.

Melvin, George. *The Post Office of British Columbia, 1858-1970.* The author, ca. 1970.

"Memories Are Made of This." *Fraser Valley Magazine*, August 23, 1976. Reprinted in *Wigwams to Windmills: A History of Ridgedale and Area.* Abbotsford, BC: Ridgedale Women's Institute, 1977.

Miller, Charles A. *Valley of the Stave.* Surrey, BC: Hancock, 1981.

Mission Community Archives. Various newspaper clippings and other information.

Nesbitt, James. "Old Homes and Families." *Colonist*, August 19, 1951.

Nesteroff, Greg. "A Ferry Tale Existence." *Nelson Star*, July 14, 2011.

Neufeldt, Robert Martens Harvey, and Ruth Derksen Siemens. *First Nations and First Settlers in the Fraser Valley, 1890–1960.* Kitchener, ON: Pandora Press, 2005.

"New Church." *Colonist*, November 6, 1874.

Nichols, Mabel. Conversation with Jean Barman, November 22, 1992.

Oblate records. Information courtesy of Irene Kelleher and Lyn Ross.

"One of Earliest Pioneers Recalls Past Pleasures." *Fraser Valley Record*, February 20, 1952.

Orchard, Imbert. *Floodland and Forest: Memories of the Chilliwack Valley.* Sound Heritage Series, no. 37. Victoria: Provincial Archives, 1983.

Orchard, Imbert. *Growing Up in the Valley: Pioneer Childhood in the Fraser Valley.* Sound Heritage Series, no. 40. Victoria: Provincial Archives, 1983.

Pengilly, Frances. "Matsqui Man Saw Valley Grow." *Vancouver Province*, February 1, 1951.

"Philip Hudson Sheffield." On https://www.familysearch.org/service/records/storage/das-mem/patron/v2/TH-904-72794-581-93/dist.txt?ctx=ArtCtxPublic. Accessed December 20, 2018.

Pierson, Jason E. *Making the White Man's West: Whiteness and the Creation of an American West.* Boulder, CO: University Press of Colorado, 2016.

"Pioneer's Death." *Colonist*, March 22, 1906.

"Pioneer Woman, Native of B.C., Buried Last Week." Unidentified clipping, February 1949. Mission Community Archives.

Powell, I., to Superintendent of Indian Affairs, Victoria, March 3, 1885. In RG 10, vol. 3694, file 14676, reel C-10121, BC Archives.

Queen's Avenue Methodist Church, New Westminster. Baptismal, marriage, and death records. United Church, BC Conference, Archives.

Ravicz, Marilyn, Diane Battung, and Laura Buker. "Rainbow Women of the Fraser Valley: Lifesongs Through the Generations." In *Not Just Pin Money: Selected Essays on the History of Women's Work in British Columbia,* ed. Barbara K. Latham and Robert J. Pazdro. Victoria: Camosun College, 1984, 37–52.

"Receive Many Congratulations." *Abbotsford, Sumas and Matsqui News*, January 21, 1948.

Reimer, Chad. *Before We Lost the Lake: A Natural and Human History of Sumas Valley*. Halfmoon Bay, BC: Caitlin Press, 2018.

Riggins, Loretta R., and Len Walker. *The Heart of the Fraser Valley: Memories of an Era Past*. Abbotsford, BC: Matsqui/Abbotsford Community Services, and Clearbrook, BC: Matsqui Centennial Society, 1991.

"River Boats Main Link to Coast." *The Progress*, June 25, 1958.

Robertson, Betty, Catherine Marcellus, and Betty Dandy. *Mission's Living Memorials*. Altona, MB: Friesen, 1992.

Ross, Lyn. Conversation, October 9, 1993.

St. Andrew's Catholic Church, Victoria. Baptismal, marriage, and death records, 1849–1934. British Columbia Archives, Add. Ms. 1.

St. Ann's Academy, New Westminster. "Register, 1865–1920." St. Ann's Archive, Victoria, relocated to Provincial Archives of British Columbia.

Schape, David M., ed. *Being Ts'elxwéyeqw: First Peoples' Voices and History from the Chilliwack-Fraser, British Columbia*. Madeira Park, BC: Harbour Publishing for the Ts'elxwéyeqw Tribe, 2017.

Sherwood, Philip, ed. *Matsqui–Sumas–Abbotsford: Pioneer Stories, 1890–1950*. MSA Museum Society, 2013.

Skinner, Constance Lindsay. Papers. Manuscripts and Archives Division, New York Public Library.

Sleigh, Daphne. *Discovering Deroche: From Nicomen to Lake Errock*. Abbotsford, BC: Abbotsford Printing, 1983.

Sleigh, Daphne. *The People of the Harrison*. Abbotsford, BC: Abbotsford Printing, 1990.

Sleigh, Daphne, adapted by. *Mission as It Was*. Mission, BC: Mission District Historical Society, 2017.

"Survivor of 1894 Flood Sandbags Matsqui Dykes." *Vancouver Sun*, undated. Copy courtesy of Irene Kelleher.

Tarasoff, Koozma J. *Plakun Trava: The Doukhobors*. Grand Forks, BC: Mir, 1982.

"Teacher Retires after 41 Years," July 12 and 19, 1950, unsourced. Reprinted in *Wigwams to Windmills: A History of Ridgedale and Area.* Abbotsford, BC: Ridgedale Women's Institute, 1977, 117.

University of the Fraser Valley. Civic Web. "President's Report to the Board," included in University College of the Fraser Valley, Board Meeting, February 3, 1999, at https://ufv.civicweb.net/document/11203. Accessed October 12, 2018.

Waite, Donald E. *The Langley Story Illustrated: An Early History of the Municipality of Langley.* Altona, MB: D.W. Friesen, 1977.

Watson, Bruce McIntyre. *Lives Lived West of the Divide: A Biographical Dictionary of Fur Traders Working West of the Rockies, 1793–1858.* Kelowna, BC: Centre for Social, Spatial, and Economic Justice, University of British Columbia, 2010.

Watt, K.J. *High Water: Living with the Fraser Floods.* Abbotsford, BC: Dairy Industry Historical Society of British Columbia, 2006.

Weir, Betty. "The Edwards Family." Undated typescript in Mission Community Archives.

Wells, Oliver N. *The Chilliwacks and Their Neighbours.* Vancouver: Talonbooks, 1987.

Wells Family. Notes in Mission Community Archives.

Where All Trails Meet. Matsqui, Sumas and Abbotsford Centennial Historical Committee, 1958.

Whitlow, Elizabeth M. "Usk." "Usk, BC," http://www.terracelibrary.ca/history1/usk_history/usk_history.htm.

Wigwams to Windmills: A History of Ridgedale and Area. Abbotsford, BC: Ridgedale Women's Institute, 1977.

Woodcock, George, and Ivan Avakumovic. *The Doukhobors.* Toronto: Oxford University Press, 1968.

Younging, Gregory. *Elements of Indigenous Style: A Guide for Writing By and About Indigenous Peoples.* Edmonton: Brush, 2018.

ABOUT THE AUTHOR

Photo Laura Sawchuk

Jean Barman is an award-winning historian and author of over a dozen books about British Columbian and Canadian history. Much of her writing attends to the stories and histories of Indigenous Peoples and to Canadian women and families. Her writing has garnered over a dozen Canadian and American awards, including the Governor General's History Award for Scholarly Research. She is professor emeritus at the University of British Columbia, a fellow of the Royal Society of Canada and the recipient of a Queen Elizabeth II Diamond Jubilee Medal. She holds graduate degrees from Harvard University, the University of California at Berkeley and University of British Columbia, and an honorary doctorate from Vancouver Island University. Jean lives in Vancouver, BC.